PLANNED
BEHAVIOR

PLANNED BEHAVIOR

The Relationship between Human Thought and Action

Christopher J. Armitage
Julie Christian
editors

Routledge
Taylor & Francis Group

LONDON AND NEW YORK

Originally published as a special issue of Current Psychology, Vol. 22, No. 3, Fall 2003.

Published 2004 by Transaction Publishers

Published 2017 by Routledge
2 Park Square, Milton Park, Abingdon, Oxon OX14 4RN
711 Third Avenue, New York, NY 10017, USA

Routledge is an imprint of the Taylor & Francis Group, an informa business

Library of Congress Number: 2004047897

Library of Congress Cataloging-in-Publication Data

Planned behavior : the relationship between human thought and action / Christopher J. Armitage and Julie Christian, editors.
    p. cm.
Includes bibliographical references and index.
ISBN 0-7658-0578-2 (alk. paper)
1. Attitude (Psychology) 2. Human behavior. 3. Prediction (Psychology)
I. Armitage, Christopher J., 1973- II. Christian, Julie.

BF327.P48   2004
153.8—dc22   2004047897

ISBN 13: 978-0-7658-0578-2 (pbk)

1

From Attitudes to Behavior: Basic and Applied Research on the Theory of Planned Behavior

Christopher J. Armitage and Julie Christian

Introduction

The social psychological study of attitudes has been one of the core areas of the discipline for decades, described by Allport (1935) as "probably the most distinctive and indispensable concept in contemporary American social psychology" (p. 798). Allport's view was based on two observations. The first was an assessment of the social psychological literature of the time, which revealed that, "No other term appears more frequently in the experimental and theoretical literature" (p. 798, Allport, 1935). The second observation was perhaps more important: Allport (1935) argued that the number of functions that attitudes served made the concept indispensable.[1] Indeed, research into the myriad functions that attitudes serve continues to be, and is arguably the fastest-growing area of attitude research (see Maio & Olson, 2000). However, research into one function of attitudes accounts for the vast majority of the psychological literature in this area: that attitudes serve to guide people's behavior.

Historically attitudes had been assumed to be predictive of behavior, although this assumption was often held in the face of compelling evidence to the contrary. Perhaps the most widely cited example of the discrepancy between attitudes and behavior is LaPiere's (1934) study. LaPiere (1934) took an extensive tour of the United States in the company of a young Chinese couple. At the time, there was much anti-Chinese sentiment and so (unknown to his companions) LaPiere (1934) made notes of the way in which they were treated. During their travels, LaPiere and his companions visited 250 establishments, yet on only one occasion were they refused service. When LaPiere (1934) subsequently wrote to the same establishments, 118 (of the 128 replies) said they would *not* accept members of the Chinese race as guests at their establishment. LaPiere (1934) concluded that there was a large gap between attitudes and behavior, and that questionnaire data could not always be trusted to be reliable. Corey (1937) also sought to address this issue directly and used a highly reliable measure to assess attitudes toward cheating, yet found a correlation of only ($r = .02$) between attitude and an objective measure of behavior. In reviewing the literature in this area, Wicker (1969) examined forty-two studies, finding that attitudes generally correlated only $r = .15$ with behaviors, and that the correlations rarely exceeded $r = .30$. Wicker (1969) concluded: "taken as a whole, these studies suggest that it is considerably more likely that attitudes will be unrelated or only very slightly related to overt behaviors than that attitudes will be closely related to actions" (p. 64).

In our view, Wicker's (1969) review can be regarded as the point at which social psychologists lost interest in simply noting the relationship between attitudes and behavior, and began examining in depth the circumstances under which attitudes were predictive of behavior. Thus, social psychologists interested in attitude-behavior relations responded to Wicker's (1969) review by looking at several "third-variable" explanations, namely, whether there were as-yet-unmeasured variables that could explain why there was not a direct relationship between attitudes and behavior. In other words, attitude-behavior researchers began to investigate potential moderators and mediators of the attitude-behavior relationship (see Baron & Kenny, 1986). The following section briefly considers potential moderators, before turning to consider *behavioral intention*, regarded as the key mediator of attitude-behavior relations.

Moderators of the Attitude-Behavior Relationship

One approach to understanding the circumstances under which attitudes do predict behavior, has been to test potential *moderators* of the attitude-behavior relationship. A moderator variable "partitions a focal independent variable into subgroups that establish its domains of maximal effectiveness in regard to a given dependent variable" (p. 1173, Baron & Kenny, 1986). In terms of the attitude-behavior relationship, attitude strength is regarded as a key moderator variable: stronger attitudes are likely to be more predictive of people's behavior than are weak attitudes. In recent years more than a dozen facets of attitude strength have been tested, several of which have been found to moderate the attitude-behavior relationship. For example, attitudes are generally more predictive of subsequent behavior if they are: univalent rather than ambivalent (e.g., Conner & Sparks, 2002), accessible in memory (e.g., Kokkinaki & Lunt, 1998), or are personally involving (e.g., Thomsen, Borgida, & Lavine, 1995).[2]

A related area has examined the moderating influence of measurement on attitude-behavior relations. Most notable in this area is the work of Fishbein and Ajzen (1975) and their *principle of correspondence* (see also Ajzen & Fishbein, 1977). In an example we used earlier, Corey (1937) tried to address the issue of measurement reliability by using an established and reliable attitude scale, yet found an attitude-behavior correlation of only $r = .02$. Fishbein and Ajzen (1975) noted that unreliability of measurement was only one possible explanation for the discrepancy between the prediction of intention and that of behavior. In particular, Fishbein and Ajzen (1975) noted that often, very global attitudes (e.g., attitude to religion) were used to predict very specific actions (e.g., attending church), and argued that wherever possible, measures of attitude and behavior should match one another in terms of action, time, target and context. That is, an individual's attitude toward exercising (action), to get fit (target), in the gym (context), in the next week (time), should be more closely related to a measure of behavior designed to tap exercising to get fit in the gym in the preceding week, than (say) an index of fitness. Consistent with this view, there are now numerous studies showing that when measures of attitude and behavior correspond, the correlation between the two is greater. For example, Davidson and Jaccard (1979) found that general attitudes to contraception were poor predictors of birth control pill use ($r = .08$) compared with a more specific measure of attitude ($r = .57$). Moreover, in a meta-analysis of eight studies that manipulated level of correspondence, Kraus (1995) found that "specific attitudes were significantly better predictors of specific behaviors than were general attitudes (combined $p < .0000001$)" (p. 64). It is notable that the empirical studies in this volume have all taken pains to adhere to this principle of correspondence.

In sum, a variety of moderators of the attitude-behavior relationship have been tested. Both attitude strength and the way in which attitudes and behaviors are measured seem to affect the magnitude of the attitude-behavior relationship. However, one problem with research into attitude strength is that there are many different measures of attitude strength, which seem to act independently of one another. For example, in three independent studies Krosnick, Boninger, Chuang, Berent, and Carnot (1993) tested as many as thirteen different indices of attitude strength, with the goal of determining a coherent structure. The authors concluded that, "...we were unable to detect any stable structure underlying these correlations. Exploratory factor analyses did not produce reliable evidence of a relational framework underlying these dimensions" (p. 1143, Krosnick et al., 1993). The implication is that there is some way to go in understanding the effects of attitude strength on attitude-behavior relations, and that further research is required. Alternatively, one could argue that to further understanding about attitude-behavior relations, one should consider factors that might mediate the relationship between attitudes and behavior. We address this issue in the following section.

"There's Only One Mediator, One Mediator": The Role of Behavioral Intentions in the Attitude-Behavior Relationship

The second approach to understanding attitude-behavior relations is to examine variables that might mediate the attitude-behavior relationship. By "mediator," we are referring to a variable "which represents the generative mechanism through which the focal independent variable is able to influence the dependent variable of interest" (p. 1173, Baron & Kenny, 1986). As far as we are aware, only one variable has been investigated in this regard, namely, *behavioral intentions* (e.g., Fishbein & Ajzen, 1975). Behavioral intentions are regarded as a summary of the motivation required to perform a particular behavior, reflecting an individual's decision to follow a course of action, as well as an index of how hard people are willing to try and perform the behavior (Ajzen & Fishbein, 1980; Fishbein & Ajzen, 1975). The idea that behavioral intentions mediate the attitude-behavior relationship represents a significant move away from the traditional view of attitudes: rather than attitudes being related directly to behavior, attitudes only serve to direct behavior to the extent that they influence intentions. Thus, Wicker's (1969) pessimistic review of the attitude-behavior relationship might have reflected the fact that intentions are the principal proximal determinant of behavior, not attitudes (for a review see Sheeran, 2002).

The Theory of Reasoned Action

Fishbein and Ajzen's (1975) view that the influence of attitude on behavior is mediated through behavioral intentions is the cornerstone of their *theory of reasoned action*. The theory of reasoned action goes further than the inclusion of intention as a mediator of the attitude-behavior relationship, it holds that attitude is only one determinant of intention and that social pressure is also likely to determine people's intentions. Thus, within this theory of reasoned action, behavioral intentions are determined by attitudes (overall positive/negative evaluations of behavior) and the perceived social pressure from significant others, *subjective norms*.

Fishbein's (1967a, 1967b) work on the summative model of attitudes underpins the theory of reasoned action. Briefly, Fishbein's model holds that individuals may possess a large number of beliefs about a particular behavior, but that only a subset are likely to be salient at any one time. Thus, both attitudes and subjective norms are determined by salient underlying beliefs. Salient behavioral beliefs are held to determine attitudes. Each behavioral belief consists of two components: an outcome belief and an outcome evaluation. The outcome belief concerns beliefs about the likelihood of particular outcomes occurring, for example the perceived likelihood that one will lose weight if one diets, or the likelihood that smoking causes cancer. Outcome beliefs are weighted (multiplied) by outcome evaluations to form each behavioral belief. This is based on the rationale that only outcomes that are valued are likely to impact upon one's attitudes.

Salient normative beliefs underpin subjective norms. Consistent with behavioral beliefs, normative beliefs consist of two components: referent beliefs and motivation to comply. Again the two components are multiplied, because one is only like to experience social pressure from particular referents if one is motivated to comply with those particular referents. Consider the following example of the normative pressure underpinning Gary's intention to use a condom.

Gary's mother might want her son to use a condom every time he has sex with a new partner, but Gary is only likely to do so to the extent that he is motivated to comply with his mother (very little in this case). Similarly, Gary's latest partner also wants Gary to use a condom every time he has sex with her; in this case, however, Gary is very motivated to comply with his new partner and therefore is more likely to intend to use a condom. Within the theory of reasoned action, both behavioral and normative beliefs are summed to produce global measures of attitude and subjective norm, respectively. More commonly, however, researchers simply use global measures to provide a summary of the belief-forming process.

Several quantitative and narrative reviews provide support for the utility of the theory of reasoned action in predicting intentions and behavior (e.g., Sheppard, Hartwick, & Warshaw, 1988; van den Putte, 1991). For the prediction of behavioral intention from attitude and subjective norm, Sheppard et al. (1988) found an average multiple correlation of $R = .66$ and an average intention-behavior correlation of $r = .53$. Thus, the theory of reasoned action possesses adequate predictive validity. Interestingly, the behavioral intention construct is considered sufficiently predictive of behavior that many researchers use it as a dependent variable, assuming that intentions consistently lead to behavior (but see Sheeran, 2002).

The Theory of Planned Behavior

Although the theory of reasoned action accounted for what Cohen (1992) would describe as a "large" proportion of the variance in behavior, researchers noted that the theory of reasoned action was an effective predictor of certain classes of behavior but not others. In fact, Ajzen (1988) himself conceded that, "The theory of reasoned action was developed explicitly to deal with purely volitional behaviors" (p. 127); in other words, relatively simple behaviors, where successful performance of the behavior required only the formation of an intention. Thus, the theory of reasoned action implies that behavior is solely dependent on personal agency (i.e., the formation of an intention), and that control over behavior (e.g., personal resources or environmental determinants of behavior) is relatively unimportant.

In order to address this issue, Ajzen (1988) proposed "...a conceptual framework that addresses the problem of incomplete voli-

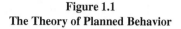

Figure 1.1
The Theory of Planned Behavior

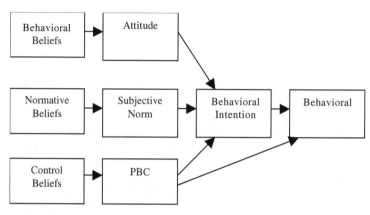

PBC= Perceived Behavioral Control

tional control" (p. 132), namely the *theory of planned behavior* (Ajzen, 1988, 1991). The theory of planned behavior (see figure 1.1) extended the theory of reasoned action by including *perceived behavioral control* as a determinant of both behavioral intention *and* behavior. The inclusion of perceived behavioral control as a predictor of behavior is based on the rationale that: holding intention constant, greater perceived control will increase the likelihood that enactment of the behavior will be successful. Further, to the extent to which perceived control reflects actual control, perceived behavioral control will directly influence behavior. Perceived behavioral control therefore acts as both a proxy measure of actual control and a measure of confidence in one's ability. Within the theory of planned behavior, perceived behavioral control is posited as a third determinant of intention: thus, the easier a behavior is, the more likely one will intend to perform it.

As with the attitude and subjective norm constructs, Ajzen posited that *control beliefs* underpin perceived behavioral control. Control beliefs are the perceived frequency of facilitating or inhibiting factors occurring by the power of those factors to inhibit/facilitate the behavior in question. Congruent with the other belief components in the theory of planned behavior, it is the control beliefs that are salient at any one time which determine global perceptions of control.

There have been several meta-analytic reviews of the theory of planned behavior, all of which have concluded that the augmentation of the theory of reasoned action with measures of perceived behavioral control has contributed significantly to the prediction of behavioral intentions and behavior (see Ajzen, 1991; Armitage & Conner, 2001; Godin & Kok, 1996). The most recent of these meta-analyses (Armitage & Conner, 2001) reviewed 185 independent studies and found that the theory of planned behavior accounted for 27 percent of the variance in subsequent behavior, and 39 percent of the variance in behavioral intentions. As predicted, perceived behavioral control added significantly to the prediction of intention and behavior, even after controlling for the effects of theory of reasoned action variables. In sum, the theory of planned behavior extends the theory of reasoned action and accounts for considerable proportion of the variance in intention and behavior. At present, the theory of planned behavior is arguably the dominant model of attitude-behavior relations.

The Special Issue

Despite considerable empirical support for the theory of planned behavior, there are still issues of debate with which researchers are currently engaged. Perhaps more so than many other theories in social psychology, research into the theory of planned behavior can properly be regarded as "action research," in so far as many of the theoretical advances have been made in relation to applied areas (Lewin, 1951). Accordingly, the chapters in this volume deal with both applied and basic research questions.

Research in the applied domain has typically examined whether the theory of planned behavior is truly a general model of social behavior by (for example) sampling diverse populations (e.g., Christian & Armitage, 2002), or by using the model to develop effective behavior change strategies (e.g., Armitage & Conner, 2002). More basic-oriented research, on the other hand has tended to focus on developing the theory of planned behavior per se. This body of research has, for example, examined potential moderators of relationships between components (e.g., Conner, Sheeran, Norman, & Armitage, 2000), as well as the predictive validity of additional variables (Conner & Armitage, 1998). With respect to the latter, Ajzen (1991) encourages the exploration of additional variables and regards the theory of planned behavior as, "...open to the inclusion of additional predictors if it can be shown that they capture a significant proportion of the variance in intention or behavior after the theory's current variables have been taken into account" (p. 199). Accordingly, most of the contributions within this volume blend applied and basic issues to great effect. The following section provides an overview of the specific contributions that appear in this volume.

As we have already noted, one of the strengths of the theory of planned behavior is its broad applicability: applications of the model can be found across numerous disciplines, including nursing, information technology, social policy and sociology. Even within psychology, research has not been restricted to the domain of social psychology: the theory of planned behavior is currently regarded as the dominant model in the field of health psychology (e.g., Armitage & Conner, 2000). Therefore, two chapters examine the generalizability of the model in two ways. First, O'Connor and Armitage report the application of an augmented theory of planned behavior to parasuicide, an area that has been relatively neglected by social psychologists, yet might benefit from a theory of planned behavior approach. O'Connor and Armitage's study provides support for the application of the theory of planned behavior to parasuicide behavior, for the inclusion of moral norm within the model, and suggests ways in which the model may be used to prevent parasuicidal behavior.

Second, Christian, Armitage, and Abrams report an application of the theory of planned behavior to homeless populations: whereas much research into the theory of planned behavior has investigated university students, much less has focused on general population samples. The Christian et al. study introduces a further innovation by examining a much-stigmatised and under-researched group, namely, homeless people. Among the challenges the study addresses is how to operationalize key constructs when the population may be unwilling or unable to complete standard measures. Moreover, the paper takes a lead from social group theorists to further examine the effects of social categorisation on norms within the theory of planned behavior.

The third chapter, by Rivis and Sheeran is a meta-analysis of the role of descriptive norms within the theory of planned behavior. Arguing that the subjective norm component accounts well for the effects of injunctive norms—but not descriptive norms—on individuals, Rivis and Sheeran review the effects of descriptive norms in the theory of planned behavior, finding that descriptive norms might usefully be included within the theory of planned behavior framework.

In the fourth chapter, Sutton, French, Hennings, Wareham, Griffin, Hardeman, and Kinmonth deal with the issue of belief elicitation. As we noted above, a key aspect of the theories of reasoned action and planned behavior is that salient underlying beliefs need to be measured. To date, very little research has addressed how this might actually be done. The Sutton et al. chapter manipulates question wording and reports on the different kinds of beliefs that are elicited. The study also tests various decision-rules for determining which beliefs are actually "salient."

The fifth contribution, from Conner, Smith and McMillan, focuses on the effects of normative pressure within the theory of planned behavior—specifically in relation to breaking the speed limit. An interesting aspect of this study is Conner et al.'s attempt to experimentally manipulate a key component of the theory of planned behavior: it has often been noted that while there is ample correlational evidence in support of the theory of planned behavior, there is actually very little experimental work in this regard (e.g., Armitage & Conner, 2001; Sutton, 1998). The researchers manipulate whether or not a passenger is present as well as the gender of the passenger, finding an interesting interaction between normative pressure, gender, and physical presence (i.e., a moderating effect).

The final chapter, by Abraham and Sheeran argues that the predictive validity of the theory of planned behavior could be enhanced with reference to goal theory. At the root of their argument is the idea that where typical theory of planned behavior studies stop (i.e., with a one-off behavior), goal theory starts, and that conceptualising behavior as part of a process that leads to higher-order goals will lead to improved intention-behavior relations.

Thus, this volume considers a full spectrum of important developments that all enhance our understanding of, and efforts to extend the theory of planned behavior. From applications through to new avenues for research, the six chapters in this volume address important issues surrounding theoretical and practical approaches to problems in attitude-intention-behavior research.

Notes

1. This quotation has also become the bane of undergraduate students taking courses in social psychology the world over—the Allport (1953) quotation is often embellished with a *Discuss* at the end.
2. Readers who are interested in this area of research should consult Petty and Krosnick's (1995) volume, *Attitude strength: Antecedents and consequences*."

References

Ajzen, I. (1988). *Attitudes, personality and behavior.* Milton Keynes, UK: Open University Press.

Ajzen, I. (1991). The theory of planned behavior. *Organizational Behavior and Human Decision Processes, 50,* 179-211.

Ajzen, I., & Fishbein, M. (1977). Attitude-behavior relations: a theoretical analysis and review of empirical research. *Psychological Bulletin, 84,* 888-918.

Ajzen, I., & Fishbein, M. (1980). *Understanding attitudes and predicting social behavior.* Englewood Cliffs, NJ: Prentice-Hall.

Allport, G. W. (1935). Attitudes. In C. Murchison (Ed.), *A handbook of social psychology* (pp. 798-844). Worcester, MA: Clark University Press.

Armitage, C. J., & Conner, M. (2000). Social cognition models and health behaviour: A structured review. *Psychology and Health, 15,* 173-189.

Armitage, C. J., & Conner, M. (2001). Efficacy of the theory of planned behaviour: A meta-analytic review. *British Journal of Social Psychology, 40,* 471-499.

Armitage, C. J., & Conner, M. (2002). Reducing fat intake: Interventions based on the theory of planned behaviour. In D. Rutter & L. Quine (Eds.), *Changing health behaviour: Intervention and research with social cognition models* (pp. 87-104). Buckingham, UK: Open University Press.

Baron, R. M., & Kenny, D. A. (1986). The moderator-mediator variable distinction in social psychological research: Conceptual, strategic, and statistical considerations. *Journal of Personality and Social Psychology, 51,* 1173-1182.

Christian, J., & Armitage, C.J. (2002). Attitudes and intentions of homeless persons towards service provision in South Wales. *British Journal of Social Psychology, 41,* 219-231.

Cohen, J. (1992). A power primer. *Psychological Bulletin, 112,* 155-159.

Conner, M., & Armitage, C. J. (1998). Extending the theory of planned behaviour: A review and avenues for further research. *Journal of Applied Social Psychology, 28,* 1429-1464.

Conner, M., Sheeran, P., Norman, P., & Armitage, C. J. (2000). Temporal stability as a moderator of relationships in the theory of planned behaviour. *British Journal of Social Psychology, 39,* 469-493.

Conner, M., & Sparks, P. (2002). Ambivalence and attitudes. *European Review of Social Psychology, 12,* 37-70.

Corey, S. M. (1937). Professed attitudes and actual behavior. *Journal of Educational Psychology, 28,* 271-280.

Davidson, A. R., & Jaccard, J. J. (1979). Variables that moderate the attitude-behavior relation: Results of a longitudinal survey. *Journal of Personality and Social Psychology, 37,* 1364-1376.

Fishbein, M. (1967a). Attitude and the prediction of behavior. In M. Fishbein (Ed.), *Readings in attitude theory and measurement* (pp. 477-492). New York: Wiley.

12   Planned Behavior

Fishbein, M. (1967b). A behavior theory approach to the relations between beliefs about an object and the attitude toward the object. In M. Fishbein (Ed.), *Readings in attitude theory and measurement* (pp. 389-400). New York: Wiley.

Fishbein, M., & Ajzen, I. (1975). *Belief, attitude, intention and behavior: An introduction to theory and research.* Reading, MA: Addison-Wesley.

Godin, G., & Kok, G. (1996). The theory of planned behavior: A review of its applications to health-related behaviors. *American Journal of Health Promotion, 11,* 87-98.

Kraus, S. J. (1995). Attitudes and the prediction of behavior: A meta-analysis of the empirical literature. *Personality and Social Psychology Bulletin, 21,* 58-75.

Kokkinaki, F., & Lunt, P. (1998). The relationship between involvement, attitude accessibility and attitude-behaviour consistency. *British Journal of Social Psychology, 36,* 497-509.

Krosnick, J. A., Boninger, D. S., Chuang, Y. C., Berent, M. K., & Carnot, C. G. (1993). Attitude strength: One construct or many related constructs? *Journal of Personality and Social Psychology, 65,* 1132-1151.

LaPiere, R. T. (1934). Attitudes vs. actions. *Social Forces, 13,* 230-237.

Lewin, K. (1951). *Field theory in social science: Selected theoretical papers.* New York: Harper.

Maio, G. R., & Olson, J. M. (2000). *Why we evaluate: Functions of attitudes.* London: Lawrence Erlbaum Associates.

Sheeran, P. (2002). Intention-behavior relations: A conceptual and empirical review. *European Review of Social Psychology, 12,* 1-36.

Sheppard, B. H., Hartwick, J., & Warshaw, P. R. (1988). The theory of reasoned action: A meta-analysis of past research with recommendations for modifications and future research. *Journal of Consumer Research, 15,* 325-343.

Sutton, S. (1998). Explaining and predicting intentions and behavior: How well are we doing? *Journal of Applied Social Psychology, 28,* 1318-1339.

Thomsen, C. J., Borgida, E., & Lavine, H. (1995). The causes and consequences of personal involvement. In R. E. Petty & J. A. Krosnick (Eds.), *Attitude strength: Antecedents and consequences* (pp. 191-214). Mahwah, NJ: Lawrence Erlbaum Associates.

van den Putte, B. (1991). *Twenty years of the theory of reasoned action of Fishbein and Ajzen: A meta-analysis.* Unpublished manuscript, University of Amsterdam.

Wicker, A. W. (1969). Attitudes versus actions: The relationship of verbal and overt behavioral responses to attitude objects. *Journal of Social Issues, 25,* 41-78.

2

Theory of Planned Behavior and Parasuicide: An Exploratory Study

Rory C. O'Connor and Christopher J. Armitage

Introduction

Parasuicide, defined as any non-fatal act in which an individual deliberately causes self-injury or ingests a substance in excess of any prescribed or generally recognised dosage (Kreitman, 1977), represents a significant personal, social and economic problem. For too many years, the rates of parasuicide and completed suicide have been increasing, especially suicide among young men. Despite research attempts, we are no closer to arresting this phenomenon than we were a decade ago. This may be for a number of reasons, however, two issues are probably central. First, suicidal behavior should be considered along a continuum, as much of the work carried out to date views deliberate self-harm[1] and completed suicide as separate phenomena, or at best as overlapping populations. As a result, research into these areas has been polarised to some degree and has not benefited from an integrated standpoint. For example, somewhere in the region of 40 percent of completed suicides have a history of self-injury, irrespective of whether, at attempt, they intended to kill themselves (O'Connor & Sheehy, 2000)—for this reason itself suicidal behavior should be considered in terms of a continuum.

Second, suicidal behavior remains stigmatised and is still firmly rooted in the domain of "abnormal" behavior. At the very best this is unfortunate, and at the worst, this represents a hindrance to (i) research per se, not to mention (ii) those who are vulnerable to sui-

Author's Note: Thanks to Hazel Connery for her assistance at the data collection stage of the study. For the purposes of this paper, deliberate self-harm, parasuicide and self-injury are used interchangeably.

cide, but who will not avail of the existing healthcare services for fear of stigma (O'Connor et al., 2000). Suicidal behavior, irrespective of how you define normality, should not be considered abnormal. Thus far, research has focused on suicide as a disease, reinforcing the notion that mental illness is a precursor to all suicidal behavior—it is not. The traditional "face" of suicidal behavior is changing, it now seems that more of those who kill themselves have not acquired a psychiatric diagnosis or been in contact with the healthcare services (O'Connor et al., 1999).

With the biopsychosocial model in the ascendance, treating suicidal behavior as the unfortunate end product in a series of interactions between normal psychological and psychosocial processes is long overdue. To this end, social cognition models have enjoyed a revival in recent years (see Armitage & Conner, 2000), their underlying premise being that we can identify predictive behavior patterns, and hence, devise interventions to modify behaviors and thus enhance well-being. Such a paradigm views behavior, be that engaging in unsafe sexual practices or smoking, as "normal" behavior. That they are both "risk-taking" behaviors, in the same way as suicidal behavior, is consistently overlooked. They differ only in timeliness of the outcome—suicidal behavior has a proximal outcome (e.g., admission to hospital / death) whereas smoking or unsafe sexual practices have distal outcomes (e.g., cancer, sexually transmitted disease).

A number of social cognition models have been designed to predict health-related behavior (e.g., health belief model, protection motivation theory, see Conner & Norman, 1996). For the purposes of the present study, the theories of reasoned action (Fishbein & Ajzen, 1975) and planned behavior (Ajzen, 1991) will be applied to the study of parasuicide. The choice of these models is based on three rationales. First, the theories of reasoned action and planned behavior have been applied widely in both health and non-health based contexts (see Ajzen, 1991; Armitage & Conner, 2001). Given that our position regards suicide as one end of a continuum of "normal" behavior, these theories provide general models of social behavior that do not focus on *illness*. Second, both reviews and empirical comparisons have demonstrated that the theories of reasoned action and planned behavior have superior predictive power when compared with other models of health behavior (e.g., Armitage &

Conner, 2000; Quine, Rutter, & Arnold, 1998). Third, Shneidman's (1996) model of suicide behavior identifies the expression of an intention to commit suicide (however it is perceived by others) as an important part of the process. The ability to predict an individual's intention to engage in deliberate self-harm therefore has considerable implications for suicide prevention.

Within the theory of reasoned action (TRA; Ajzen & Fishbein, 1980; Fishbein & Ajzen, 1975), behavioral intention is regarded as the proximal determinant of behavior. Behavioral intention is regarded as the motivation necessary to engage in a particular behavior: the greater one's intention to (for example) commit suicide, the more likely one is to actually engage in this act. The predictive power of behavioral intention has been demonstrated in a number of meta-analyses (e.g., Armitage & Conner, 2001; Randall & Wolff, 1994; Sheeran & Orbell, 1998), and many studies use measures of behavioral intention as a proxy for actual behavior, where such measures would be inappropriate or difficult to obtain (e.g., Abrams, Hinkle, & Tomlins, 1999; Liao, Shao, Wang, & Chen, 1999). In turn, behavioral intentions are independently determined by attitudes and subjective norms. Attitudes are positive or negative evaluations of objects or behaviors, and subjective norms are measures of the perceived social pressure to engage (or not) in the behavior.

The theory of planned behavior (TPB; Ajzen, 1991) extends the TRA by including measures of perceived behavioral control. Ajzen (1991) argues that perceived behavioral control (PBC) is synonymous with Bandura's (1997) notion of self-efficacy (i.e., "confidence in one's own ability"). Thus, where individuals believe that a particular behavior is under their personal control, the more likely they are to both intend to engage in that behavior, and also to actually perform that behavior. Several meta-analyses support the inclusion of PBC to extend the TRA, both in relation to health behaviors (Godin & Kok, 1996) and social behavior in general (Ajzen, 1991; Armitage & Conner, 2001).

However, in spite of broad support for the TPB, it has been argued that it might be possible to increase the predictive power of the model by incorporating additional variables (e.g., Conner & Armitage, 1998). Two in particular—moral norm and anticipated affect—are analogous with constructs that have been used to distinguish suicidal sub-types (O'Connor et al., 2000).

Moral norm and anticipated affect have been shown to add to the prediction of intentions, over and above TPB variables (see Conner & Armitage, 1998; van der Pligt & de Vries, 1998). Moral norms are operationally defined as, "...*personal* feelings of...responsibility to perform, or refuse to perform, a certain behavior" (Ajzen, 1991, p. 199). Thus, moral norms are distinct from subjective norms insofar as they are feelings associated with personal norms, rather than the direct social pressure that is exerted by subjective norms. Conner and Armitage (1998) have demonstrated that moral norms account for (on average) an additional 4 percent of the variance in intention, over and above the effects of TPB variables (see also Manstead, 2000). Anticipated affect has been included within the TPB to extend the model beyond a purely rational decision making model. More specifically, this construct takes account of how individuals rate they will feel after engaging in a particular behavior (or not). These anticipated feelings are held to exert motivational significance over individuals, as evidenced by a series of studies by Richard and colleagues (e.g., Richard, van der Pligt, & de Vries, 1995, 1996), which indicate that anticipated affect accounted for additional variance in behavioral intentions, over and above TPB variables.

The aims of the present exploratory study were twofold: (a) to test the efficacy of the TPB in the domain of parasuicide and hence its efficacy as a potential screening tool; (b) examine whether anticipated affect and moral norms contribute additional variance to the prediction of behavioral intentions. Despite the relatively small sample size relative to traditional TPB applications, this study has considerable practical and theoretical utility, if successful. For example, it would add to the growing body of evidence which suggests that "suicide and attempted suicide are actions that are planned and carried out by individuals, involving conscious processes, and they are thus not mere signs of illness and pathology" (Michel & Valach, 2001, p.230). It would also provide an alternative framework on which to base therapeutic technologies derived from the sphere of normal rather than abnormal psychological functioning.

Method

Participants

Patients admitted overnight to the acute receiving wards of a Glasgow hospital were considered for inclusion in the study. This included patients presenting with minor physical ailments as well as those presenting with an episode of deliberate self-harm (ICD codes X60-X84). During the study period, eleven parasuicide patients, and thirty-three hospital controls were tested. This did not represent a consecutive sample but rather reflected the practical limitations of recruiting patients admitted via a general hospital. Eleven non-hospital controls, drawn from an opportunistic sample, were assessed on the same measures as the inpatients (as described in MacLeod et al., 1993). The mean ages of the groups differed significantly (Kruskall-Wallis one way ANOVA, $p<.05$): parasuicides 32.64 yrs (SD=11.70), hospital controls 41.33 yrs (SD=12.55) and non-hospital controls 29.91 yrs (SD=12.65). The distribution of gender (twenty-seven males and twenty-eight females in total) and marital status was similar for each of the groups.

Some individuals in the control groups had self-harmed in the past, hence the participants were also classified into "ever" self-harmers ($n=21$) and "never" self-harmers ($n=34$). No statistically significant differences were noted across the groups in terms of gender, age or marital status. The mean ages of the "ever" self-harmers and "never" self-harmers were (mean = 33.62 yrs; SD = 12.44) and (39.59 yrs; SD = 13.29) respectively.

Measures

Behavioral intention. Behavioral intention was measured using three items measured on bipolar (-3 to +3) scales: "I intend to deliberately harm myself in the future (definitely do not-definitely do)," "I expect I will deliberately harm myself in the future (definitely will not-definitely will)," and "I *want* to deliberately harm myself in the future (definitely do not-definitely do)." The mean of the items made a scale with good internal reliability (Cronbach's $\propto = .72$).

Attitude. The global measure of attitude was assessed by taking the mean to the statement, "My deliberately harming myself is...." This statement was evaluated on six 7-point bipolar (-3 to +3) scales with the endpoints: bad-good, harmful-beneficial, unpleasant-pleasant, negative-positive, unenjoyable-enjoyable, and useless-useful. The Cronbach's $\propto$ for the scale was .81.

Subjective norm. Perceived social pressure to deliberately self-harm was assessed using responses to the item, "People who are important to me think I (should not deliberately harm myself-should deliberately harm myself)." This was measured on a unipolar (+1 to +7) scale.

Self-efficacy. Confidence in one's own ability was assessed using the responses to three items: "I believe I have the ability to deliberately harm myself in the future (definitely do not-definitely do), "To what extent do you see yourself as being capable of deliberately harming yourself in the future? (very incapable of harming myself-very capable of harming myself)," and "How confident are you that you will be able to deliberately harm yourself in the future? (not very confident-very confident)." Cronbach's ∝ indicated good internal reliability for the scale (a = .84).

Moral norm. Moral norm was measured using three 7-point unipolar scales, all the "strongly disagree-strongly agree" endpoints. The items were: "It would be morally wrong for me to deliberately harm myself," "Deliberately harming myself goes against my principles," and "I personally feel I have a moral obligation *not* to deliberately harm myself." Cronbach's a for the scale was .73.

Anticipated affect. Three items were used to measure anticipated feelings following deliberate self-harm. A statement was presented ("If I deliberately harmed myself, I would feel…"), followed by three antonymous adjectives: *feeble-strong, tense-relaxed* and *sad-happy.* The scale was internally reliable (Cronbach's ∝ = .77).

Procedure

All participants were given a brief introduction outlining the nature of their participation and the study aims. We highlighted the voluntary nature of participation and, in the cases of the hospital participants, patients were assured that non-participation would not interfere with their treatment protocol. Ethical approval was obtained from the University Hospital Trust and University Psychology Department. Demographic details were acquired from hospital records and during the testing procedure. All participants completed the questionnaire, as outlined above, to assess the components of the TPB and additional variables. To enhance anonymity and to reduce response bias, all participants were given an envelope to deposit their questionnaire, on completion.

Analysis

In order to test the applicability of the TPB in this area, we adopted two strategies. The first utilised TPB variables to discriminate between cases of parasuicide and hospital and normal controls. The second examined predictive validity: testing the ability of the extended TPB to predict intentions to self-harm.

Results

Table 2.1 presents the group means for TPB variables, divided into parasuicide, hospital control and control groups. The data indicate that parasuicides differed significantly from hospital controls on anticipated affect and self-efficacy, such that parasuicides were more likely to rate that self-harm would improve their mood, and that they felt more confident in their ability to harm themselves. Overall, all three groups reported that they did not intend to self-harm in the future, but the parasuicide group differed significantly from both control groups in that they were more disposed to harming themselves in the future. These data show that the TPB usefully discriminates clinical groups.

Table 2.1
Comparisons of Group Means for TPB and Additional Variables:
Parasuicide Compared with Two Control Groups

Variables	Parasuicide ($n = 11$)	Hospital Controls ($n = 33$)	Controls ($n = 11$)
Anticipated Affect	3.48 (1.67)[a]	1.85 (1.61)[b]	2.33 (1.71)[ab]
Attitude	-2.29 (0.81)	-2.68 (0.75)	-2.35 (1.20)
Behavioral intention	-1.33 (1.99)[a]	-2.81 (0.49)[b]	-2.33 (1.20)[b]
Moral Norm	5.79 (1.62)	5.40 (2.11)	5.61 (1.58)
Subjective Norm	1.00 (0.00)	1.42 (1.48)	1.09 (0.30)
Self-efficacy	4.67 (2.39)[a]	2.21 (1.79)[b]	3.76 (2.58)[ac]

Note. Means with different superscripts differ significantly at the .05 level using Newman-Keuls *post hoc* pairwise comparisons. Re-analysis using Kruskal-Wallis one-way ANOVA, produced identical results. Significant between-groups differences were found for: anticipated affect (c^2 [2] = 10.65, $p < .01$), behavioral intention (c^2 [2] = 8.45, $p < .05$), and self-efficacy (c^2 [2] = 10.52, $p < .01$).

However, the data presented in table 2.1 includes only those participants who presented at hospital for treatment. In the community there are many who self-harm but do not present for treatment. We therefore divided the sample into two groups: those who had never self-harmed (n = 34) and those who had self-harmed at least once in the past (n = 21). The groups differed significantly on all measured variables (see table 2.2). More specifically, prior self-harmers were more positively disposed to self-harming; more likely to intend to self-harm in the future; felt more social pressure to self-harm, and perceived greater self-efficacy with respect to their self-harming. Moreover, prior self-harmers reported that self-harming in the future would make them feel more calm, and that self-harming was less morally wrong. Thus, the data suggest that in the community at large, there may be people that are disposed to self-harm and that the TPB may be a useful tool for identifying them.

Table 2.2
Comparisons of Group Means for TPB and Additional Variables:
Ever Self-Harmed versus Never Self-Harmed

Variables	Ever Self-Harmed ($n = 21$)	Never Self-Harmed ($n = 34$)
Anticipated Affect	2.86 (1.42)	1.92 (1.84)
Attitude	-2.03 (1.10)	-2.85 (0.49)
Behavioral Intention	-1.57 (1.64)	-2.94 (0.21)
Moral Norm	4.85 (1.66)	5.93 (1.95)
Subjective Norm	1.71 (1.82)	1.00 (0.00)
Self-Efficacy	4.63 (2.17)	2.01 (1.74)

Note. Groups differ significantly at the .05 level using both parametric and non-parametric (Kruskal-Wallis) one-way ANOVA. F statistics for the ANOVA ranged from 3.95 to 24.43 (dfs = 1, 53); c^2's for the Kruskal-Wallis tests ranged from 6.85 to 21.89 (dfs = 1).

The second stage of the analysis focused on the predictive utility of the TPB. Table 2.3 shows intercorrelations between TPB and additional variables. There were significant positive attitude-intention and self-efficacy-intention correlations but not so for subjective norm and intention. The moral norm and anticipated affect-behavioral intention correlations were also not significant, although moral norm was significantly negatively correlated with attitudes, subjective norm and self-efficacy.

Table 2.3
Zero-Order Correlations between Measured Variables

	Att	SN	SE	BI	MN	A
Attitude (Att)	—					
Subjective Norm (SN)	.22	—				
Self-Efficacy (SE)	.48**	-.09	—			
Behavioral Intention (BI)	.58**	.06	.62**	—		
Moral Norm (MN)	-.46**	-.30*	-.25*	-.10	—	
Anticipated Affect (A)	.16	-.03	.21	.16	-.18	—

$*p < .05.$ $**p < .01.$

Table 2.4
Hierarchical Regression Analyses of Expanded TPB Variables

Step/Predictor Regression on Intention	R	R^2	ΔR^2	F for change	β at Step	Final β
1. Attitude	.57	.33	.33	11.49***	.60***	.44**
Subjective Norm					-.08	.05
2. Self-Efficacy	.69	.48	.15	13.27***	.45***	.47***
3. Anticipated Affect	.73	.53	.05	2.53	.05	.05
Moral Norm					.27*	.27*

$*p < .05.$ $**p < .01.$ $***p < .001.$

Table 2.4 presents hierarchical regression analysis of extended TPB variables on behavioral intentions. Attitude and subjective norm were entered on step 1. Together, these variables accounted for a significant proportion (33 percent) of the variance in intention, although subjective norm was a non-significant predictor. Self-efficacy was entered on step 2, accounting for significant additional variance (R^2change = .15, p < .001), thus indicating support for the extension of the theory of reasoned action. The inclusion of moral norm and anticipated affect on the final step accounted for an additional 5 percent of the variance, with moral norm being the only predictor (R^2change = .05, p<.05). The present findings provide support not only for the TPB as applied to parasuicide, but also for the addition of moral norm.

Discussion

The aims of this study were two-fold: to test the efficacy of the TPB in the domain of parasuicide and hence its efficacy as a potential screening tool; to examine whether anticipated affect and moral norms contribute additional variance to the prediction of behavioral intentions. To our knowledge, this is the first study to apply the TPB to suicidal behavior.

Findings from this study support the efficacy of the TPB in the domain of parasuicide and support the notion that deliberate self-harm can be explained in terms of "normal" psychological constructs. All the TPB variables together with anticipated affect and moral norms discriminated between those who had ever self-harmed and those who had never self-harmed. Moreover, TPB variables explained almost 50 percent of the variance associated with intention to deliberately self-harm, with moral norm (but not anticipated affect) explaining additional variance. This provides support for our extension of the TPB (see also Conner & Armitage, 1998; Manstead, 2000).

The UK government recently identified the reduction of death from suicide as a priority area earmarked for particular attention, it hopes "to reduce the death rate from suicide and undetermined injury by at least a further sixth by 2010"(Our Healthier Nation, Secretary of State for Health, 1998, p.78). To this end, the present findings afford a new perspective for the study and treatment of suicidal individuals that ought to assist in combating deliberate self-harm and completed suicide. The implications of these findings are considerable—here we focus on two in particular.

The first implication concerns the successful application of a social cognition model (i.e., TPB): this supports our premise that suicidal behavior ought to be considered within the domain of health as well as clinical psychology (O'Connor & Sheehy, 2001). This enhances our understanding of the suicidal process, helps to destigmatize suicide and roots it firmly within the domain of everyday behavior thus reducing its taboo status. Moreover, it extends applications of the TPB beyond health behaviors that involve relatively distal health outcomes (e.g., exercise, cigarette smoking) to a behavior that is both extreme and immediate.

The second major implication is that this study provides a novel framework for identifying and treating suicidal individuals. At-risk patients could be assessed along these variables, effectively screening those who present with "high-risk" characteristics. In addition to the existing treatment protocols, interventions could be developed to modify individual attitudes and beliefs thereby reducing risk. By way of an example, the present study found that subjective norms and anticipated affect exerted very little influence on parasuicide intentions. In contrast, attitudes and self-efficacy were the dominant predictors of behavioral intention, and might therefore provide useful strategies for intervention. Both self-efficacy and attitudes are rooted in behavioral decision-making insofar as they are determined by beliefs concerning the likelihood of certain outcomes (see Bandura, 1997; Fishbein & Ajzen, 1975). Thus, techniques that focus on the restructuring of cognitions (e.g., cognitive behavioral therapy) might be more successful than attempts to focus on feelings or social environment (e.g., psychodynamic approaches). These data are therefore suggestive of the fact that the decision to self-harm may be largely rational, if not logical. Further research is required to investigate these proposals.

Albeit that these findings support the utility of TPB in explaining suicidal behavior, they ought to be replicated with a larger sample employing a longitudinal study design, to determine whether the TPB can predict those individuals who actually engage in suicidal behavior in the future. No research to date has been able to do this was any degree of sensitivity or specificity (see Pokorny, 1993). It is alarming that the best predictor of completed suicide is history of previous suicide attempt. Further research is therefore required to identify the variables that mediate the relationship between past behavior and future behavior. This type of work has been one of the focuses of research in social cognition models (see Armitage & Conner, 2000).

In summary, this study has demonstrated that deliberate self-harm, the best predictor of suicide, can be explained within a social cognition framework, specifically that the measurement of attitudes, subjective norm, self-efficacy, moral norms and anticipated affect differentiate, cross-sectionally, those individuals with and without a history of self-harm. The challenge now is to apply the TPB prospectively, and if successful, this will serve as the foundation for developing an attitude-based screening tool for parasuicide.

References

Abrams, D., Hinkle, S., & Tomlins, M. (1999). Leaving Hong Kong?: The roles of attitude, subjective norm, perceived control, social identity and relative deprivation. *International Journal of Intercultural Relations, 23,* 319-338.

Ajzen, I. (1991). The theory of planned behavior. *Organizational Behavior and Human Decision Processes, 50,* 179-211.

Ajzen, I., & Fishbein, M. (1980). *Understanding attitudes and predicting social behavior.* Englewood Cliffs, NJ: Prentice-Hall.

Armitage, C. J., & Conner, M. (2000). Social cognition models and health behaviour: A structured review. *Psychology and Health, 15,* 173-189.

Armitage, C. J., & Conner, M. (2001). Efficacy of the theory of planned behaviour: A meta-analytic review. *British Journal of Social Psychology, 40,* 471-499.

Bandura, A. (1997). *Self-efficacy: The exercise of control.* New York: Freeman.

Conner, M., & Armitage, C. J. (1998). Extending the theory of planned behavior: A review and avenues for further research. *Journal of Applied Social Psychology,* 28, 1429-1464.

Conner, M., & Norman, P. (Eds.) (1996). *Predicting health behaviour.* Buckingham, UK: Open University Press.

Fishbein, M., & Ajzen, I. (1975). *Belief, attitude, intention and behavior: An introduction to theory and research.* Reading, MA: Addison-Wesley.

Godin, G., & Kok, G. (1996). The theory of planned behavior: A review of its applications to health-related behaviors. *American Journal of Health Promotion, 11,* 87-98.

Kreitman, N. (1977). *Parasuicide.* Chichester, UK: Wiley.

Liao, S., Shao, Y. P., Wang, H., & Chen, A. (1999). The adoption of virtual banking: an empirical study. *International Journal of Information Management, 19,* 63-74.

MacLeod, A.K., Rose, G.S. & Williams, J.M.G. (1993). Components of hopelessness about the future in parasuicide. *Cognitive Therapy & Research, 17,* 5, 441-455.

Manstead, A. S. R. (2000). The role of moral norm in the attitude-behavior relationship. In D. J. Terry & M. A. Hogg (Eds.), *Attitudes, behavior and social context: The role of norms and group membership* (pp. 11-30). London: Lawrence Erlbaum.

Michel, K. & Valach, L. (2001). Suicide as Goal-directed Action. In K van Heeringen (Ed.). *Understanding Suicidal Behaviour.* Chichester, UK: Wiley & Sons.

O'Connor, R.C. & Sheehy, N.P. (2001). State of the art: Suicidal behaviour. *The Psychologist, 14,* 20-24.

O'Connor, R.C. & Sheehy, N.P. (2000). *Understanding Suicidal Behaviour.* Leicester: BPS Books. ISBN 1 85433 290 2

O'Connor, R.C., Sheehy, N.P. & O'Connor, D.B. (2000). Fifty cases of general hospital parasuicide. *British Journal of Health Psychology*, *5*, 83-95.

O'Connor, R.C., Sheehy, N.P. & O'Connor, D.B. (1999). The classification of completed suicide into sub-types. *Journal of Mental Health*, *8* (*6*), 629-637

Pokorny, A.D. (1993). Suicide prediction revisited. *Suicide and Life-threatening Behaviour*, *23* (*1*), 1-10.

Richard, R., van der Pligt, J., & de Vries, N. (1995). Anticipated affective reactions and prevention of AIDS. *British Journal of Social Psychology*, *34*, 9-21.

Richard, R., van der Pligt, J., & de Vries, N. (1996). Anticipated affect and behavioral choice. *Basic and Applied Social Psychology*, *18*, 111-129.

Shneidman, E.S. (1996). *The Suicidal Mind*. Oxford University Press: New York.

Secretary of State for Health (1998). *Our Healthier Nation – A Contract for Health*. HMSO: London.

van der Pligt, J., & de Vries, N. K. (1998). Expectancy-value models of health behaviour: The role of salience and anticipated affect. *Psychology and Health*, *13*, 289-306.

3

Predicting Uptake of Housing Services: The Role of Self-Categorization in the Theory of Planned Behavior

Julie Christian, Christopher J. Armitage, and Dominic Abrams

Introduction

The UK government spends, on average, £11.6 billion per annum on short-term accommodation to house homeless people (Shelter, 2001). In spite of this, recent estimates suggest there are still as many as 108,000 homeless people in the UK (Social Trends, 2001; Wilcox, 2000). The implication is that alternative—preferably long-term—methods of reducing the numbers of homeless are required to address the housing issue, as well as deal with social exclusion caused by homelessness (Pleace, 1998).

One alternative to providing short-term accommodation (often in the form of bed and breakfast accommodation) is the provision of housing support services (Fitzpatrick, Kemp & Klinker, 2000; Randell & Brown, 1996). These programs are aimed at assisting homeless people acquire and maintain tenancies, as they progress into longer-term accommodation (i.e., shared housing and self-contained flats—without support). Unfortunately, such programs have not dramatically decreased the number of homeless people, because homeless people regularly discontinue their use of housing services within six

Authors' note: We thank all the homeless people and organizations that took part in this research. We are also grateful to Prof. David Clapham for extensive assistance with data collection. Portions of this article formed the basis for a Report to the Welsh Assembly, and were funded by Grant # 856-11-84, Section 180, made to the first author.

months of initial programme uptake (O'Callaghan, Dominian, Evans, Dix, Smith, Williams, & Zimmeck, 1996).

While many studies have examined *how* people become homeless (Blecher & DiBlasio, 1990; Jahiel, 1992), very little is known about what might motivate homeless people to make use of- and to persist in their use of- housing services because housing and homelessness advocacy organizations lack the resources necessary to explore the underlying basis for motivations to use services (Christian & Maio, 2001). Given the importance of these issues and the general absence of knowledge about uptake of services, we decided to explore these issues in South Wales, which has one of the fastest rising level of homelessness, and currently has a homeless population of 16,800. In sum, there is very little research into the psychological variables that facilitate and inhibit the uptake of housing services: the aim of the present research is to redress this balance.

The Relevance of TPB to Study of Homelessness

Researchers have applied both the theory of reasoned action and planned behavior to the study of homelessness with some success (Christian & Abrams, under review; Christian & Armitage, 2002; Wright, 1998). Of these studies Christian and Armitage (2002) and Christian and Abrams (under review) hold the most relevance for the present research. For example, Christian and Armitage's (2002) explored the predictive utility of the TPB within the context of housing outreaches, or programmes assisting homeless people to find accommodation. In contrast with much of the research into the TPB, Christian and Armitage (2002) found that the subjective norm was the most influential predictor of behavior, unmediated by intentions (cf. Armitage & Conner, 2001).

More recently, Christian and Abrams (under review) replicated the Christian and Armitage (2002) study, and extended it to examine further normative variables and to explore outreach uptake among homeless people in the UK. In this context, the researchers were interested in the link between formal authority, perceived social targets, TPB and behavior. Christian and Abrams (under review) found that—consistent with Christian and Armitage (2002)—behavior was most strongly predicted by subjective norm, identification with support services, attitude to authority, and to a lesser extent, attitude toward using the outreach service. Moreover, in contrast with much of the social policy literature, Christian and Abrams (under review) demonstrated that there were no distinctive effects associated with gender, marital status or age. Rather, effects associated with these variables are fully mediated by the TPB and attitude to authority measures.

The present research was designed to both replicate and extend these findings, by further investigating the direct effect of norms on behavior and examining a different type of service, namely housing support services. Housing support services aid the homeless by providing support "in the community" either as they gain access to short-term housing, or once in short-term accommodation. More specifically, these services (1) facilitate housing tenancy process; (2) provide regular visits to individuals in order to ensure that their tenancies run smoothly; and (3) offer a central place where individuals can "drop in" and gain support for a variety of activities (prior to and during tenancies). The following section outlines the theoretical approach taken in the present paper.

Theory of Planned Behavior and Social Identity

Social identity theory holds that behavior is driven by the extent to which one identifies with one's social group (e.g., Abrams & Hogg, 1990). In further understanding the concept of social identity as a motivational construct, researchers have combined social identity theory and the TPB. For example, Terry, Hogg, and White (1999) found that social identity exerted a direct effect on intention, and an indirect one on behavior. Thus, the more one identifies with one's social group, the more likely one is to intend to engage in that particular behavior. However, intentions were stronger for those who did not identify with the referent group (i.e., friends) than those who did, suggesting that one's uniqueness was more salient than one's group identification. Interestingly, the study provides some evidence that self-definition and uniqueness affect the salience of norms for role specific behaviors.

This has also been made clear in other social identity and TPB studies. In the domain of turnover intentions Abrams, Ando, and Hinkle (1998) observed that organizational identification was a more powerful predictor than intentions, and that the effects of subjective norms varied depending on the cultural context. Taken together, these studies suggest there is potential for exploring the influence of individual and group based identification variables within the framework of the TPB.

Social Identity—Self-categorization and Relevance to Homelessness

The present research therefore considers two levels of identity: self-categorization as a service user and the effect of group (or friendship) norms on uptake of housing and support services. Briefly, it is possible that the more a person seems him or herself as belonging to a category of "homeless people that use services," the more likely the individual will be to regard services as being self-relevant. Moreover, though these identifications may affect intention, it is also likely that they affect behavior directly because identity-based causes of behavior may not depend on the rational decision making process that underpin behavior as conceptualized in the TPB (cf Charng, Piliavin, & Callero, 1988). Moreover, it is plausible that self-identity (i.e., service user identity in this context) may actually be interlinked with social ideals about individualism. In such cases, self identity may reflect a wider held ideal about groups, in which case we would expect self-base social identity to be more predictive of behavior than group identity on identity based behaviors (see Jetten, Postmes, & McAuliffe, 2002).

This distinction also finds support in the homelessness literature. For example, Snow and Anderson (1987), in a study of seventy-one homeless people explored social identity and homelessness from a sociological perspective. They found that homeless people engaged in social distancing, or frequently drew important distinctions between themselves and others. That is, they expressed a desire not to be associated with other homeless people or institutions that serve them. For example, the participants suggested that they were not in the same position as "other homeless people" (e.g., "see him, I'm not like him over there. I don't do . . . .")

Similarly, Farrington and Robinson (1999) conducted unstructured interviews with twenty-one homeless people from a sheltered accommodation service near Bristol (UK). The interviews were loosely guided by the theoretical postulates of Social Identity Theory (SIT: Tajfel & Turner, 1979). On the basis of their qualitative analysis, they concluded that the role of social identification, first as a homeless person, and secondly with particular groups, diminished the longer a person had been homeless. That is, that the distinction between the levels of identification diminishes with time on "the streets." This was suggested, although on an exploratory basis, as a means for understanding use of shelter services. From the data, however, it is unclear whether Farrington and Robinson tested the distinction between types of social identit—or whether the findings might have been the function of the length of time spent an individual spent as homeless.

In both cases, however, the literature makes no attempt to understand *how* these issues might be internalized, or *what* may facilitate individuals' efforts to use housing support services. In particular there is little analysis of the impact of personal and group relationships on individuals' responses to seeking housing assistance, although there has been considerable inference about this (see Bates & Toro, 1999; Fitzpatrick, Kemp, & Klinker, 2000). From a theoretical perspective, such an analysis might explain why norms predict behavior independently of behavioral intentions (cf. Christian & Abrams, under review; Christian & Armitage, 2002).

The Present Research

The present study aims to investigate the utility of the TPB and social identity variables to predict homeless people's use of housing support services. On the basis of our previous research, we expected that stronger subjective norms would result in higher uptake of housing and support services. Moreover, based on the research reviewed above, it seems likely that the impact of service user identity, and group identity on behavior may depend on whether there are strong pressures from immediate significant others in a person's social network.

Method

Participants

The participants were 80 (M =60, F=20; Age =17-70, M=32.99, SD=11.45) homeless people taking part in housing and support services in South Wales, UK. Although this is almost ½ percent of the total homeless population in Wales, it is representative, and takes into consideration growth areas in the population. Of those participating, eight selected from overnight sheltered accommodation, twenty-five were from short-term flats or shared housing, fourteen were from drop-in centres, or "street outreaches," and thirty-three were from other longer-term housing service schemes (including supported youth schemes).

The majority (81 percent) of the sample received government benefits, and the participants were predominately: Caucasian (96 percent); males (75 percent); single persons (93 percent); previously taken part in housing support programmes, other than the programme interviewed at (43 percent); and reporting no educational achievement (85 percent) (see Anderson, 1994; Burrows, 1997; Fitzpatrick, Kemp, & Klinker, 2000).

Recruiting

Sampled from these services. Homeless people were recruited from sheltered accommodation facilities, and from locations on the streets. Were possible we also representatively sampled by names from daily registers. Also, letters were displayed in facilities explaining about the research project, and subsequently drop-in appointments were scheduled with individuals interested in taking part in the study. Additionally, the researcher also visited drop-in facilities and other accommodation both in the morning and evening, approaching potential participants, and asking if they would take part in the study. Days and times of the week were varied to ensure a more representative sample. Upon three occasions, key workers also accompanied the researcher, at the participant's request.

Measures

Pilot interviews were conducted with 16 (M = 11, F = 5) homeless people, and the resulting information was used to construct a structured interview questionnaire. The structured interview was based on the TPB and assessed the following variables. All items were coded using five-point response scales.

Behavioral intentions. Behavioral intention was measured using three items: "Do you intend to use a housing support programme in the future?" "Are you likely to use a housing support programme in the future?" "(The) chances are that you're likely to use a housing support programme in the future," scored 1 (*strongly disagree*) to 5 (*strongly agree*). The mean of the 3 items was taken as a measure of intention with the high score indicating positive intention to use the support programme ($\alpha = .85$).

Attitude. Participants were presented with the statement: "Using a housing support programme in the future would be... important/unimportant; satisfying/unsatisfying; positive/negative; useful/useless," scored 1 (*strongly disagree*) to 5 (*strongly agree*). The mean of the four items was taken as a measure of attitude with the high score indicating a positive attitude towards the use of the housing support programme ($\alpha = .92$).

Subjective norm. Participants were asked if they felt that friends and social workers influenced their decision to participate in support programmes. For example, "my social worker thinks that I should use a support programme in the future, " scored 1 (*strongly disagree*) to 5 (*strongly agree*). The mean of the two items was taken as a measure of subjective norms with the high score indicating greater influence from social referents towards support programme utilization ($\alpha = .86$).

Perceived behavioral control. Three items tapped perceived behavioral control: "It is easy for me to use a housing support programme in the future," "Whether or not I use a housing support programme in the future is entirely up to me," and "I can easily use a housing support programme in the future," scored 1 (*strongly disagree*) to 5 (*strongly agree*). The mean of the three items was taken as a measure of perceived behavioral control with the high score indicating a greater degree of perceived control towards the use of the programme ($\alpha = .92$).

Friendship group norm (FGN). Two items measured group norms, "how many of your friends use housing support programmes?" and "most of my friends would consider my use of housing support programmes (in the future) desirable," scored 1 (*none*) to 5 (*all*). The mean of the two items was taken as a measure of group norm with the high score indicating a greater influence of the normative component ($\alpha = .94$).

Friendship group identity (FGI). Participants were presented with the following two items, "how much do you identify with your mates," and "how well do you feel that you fit in with them?" Items were scored 1 (*do not identify/ do not fit in,* respectively) to 5 (*completely identify/completely fit in,* respectively). The mean of the two items was taken as a measure of group identity with the high score indicating a greater degree of identity ($\alpha = .92$).

Service user social identity (SUSI). Three items were used to assess social identity: "using housing support programmes is an important part of who I am; I am not the type of person that is orientated toward using housing support programmes; It would be a loss if I where forced to give up using housing support programme services." Items were scored 1 (*strongly disagree*) to 5 (*strongly agree*), with the mean of the three items taken as a measure of social identity (the high score indicating a greater degree of identity drawn from the use of the support programme) (α =.72).

Prior behavior. A single item was used to measure prior behavior, "Have you ever use a housing support programme before?" The item was scored 1 (*never used before*) to 5 (*have utilized services on a continual basis*). Since prior behavior was measured using a single item, no alpha coefficient was computed.

Behavior measure. Respondents' participation in a service programme was collected one year later. The data were coded as (1) no longer participating to (2) participation continued.

Procedure

All interview schedules were administered verbally and on a one to one basis to minimize the effects of illiteracy, and other factors likely to hinder rates of participation (Akilu, 1992; Christian & Armitage, 2002; Milburn, Watt, & Anderson, 1986; Toro & Wall, 1991). Participants were told at the beginning of the interview that all their responses were confidential, and that they would not affect their future use of services. Interviews took on average forty-five minutes to one hour to complete. Participants' travel expenses were reimbursed, but they were not paid for their assistance.

Results

Descriptive Analyses

Initial analysis screened for multivariate outliers and revealed four cases that were excluded from further analyses, leaving eighty cases in all. Sixty were male, twenty were single, and the mean age was thirty-three (SD = 11.45). Preliminary findings also suggested that there were discrepancies between data collection locations on "the streets" (also included here were drop-in centers) and sheltered accommodation locations. For this reason, data were compared, and t-test findings confirmed that there were significant differences between intentions to uptake behavior at time one (t = -3.56, df = 78, p <.01). However, no other differences were found suggesting that the data could be pooled, and analyses conducted.

The means, standard deviations and intercorrelations among variables are shown in table 3.1. In general, participants had a favorable view towards using housing support services programmes. For example, mean scores on intention, attitude and perceived control were greater than 4 on 5-point scales. Table 3.1 also shows significant correlations among the TPB variables. For example, significant relationships were found between behavior intentions, perceived behavioral control, self-identity, and group norms. Likewise, behavior was significantly related to subjective norms.

Determinants of Intention

Hierarchical regression analysis was used to examine the predictors of participants' intentions to use housing support service programs. The variables were entered in four blocks: (1) attitude and subjective norms; (2) perceived behavioral control; (3) prior behavior; and (4) service user social identity, friendship group norm, and friendship group identity (See table 3.2). In this way it was possible to assess the predictive utility of the TRA and TPB as well as the additional predictive utility of prior behavior, and other identity variables under consideration.

The TRA was able to explain 21 percent of the variance in intentions F (2, 73) = 1.90, p =n.s., with neither attitude nor subjective norms emerging as significant predictors. The addition of perceived behavioral control at step 2 increased the amount of variance explained by 17 percent (*F change* = 8.11 p <.01). At step 2, perceived control was a significant predictor, while attitudes and subjective norms were not. The addition of prior behavior at step 3 led to no further increment in the amount of variance explained (*F change* = .19 p = n.s.). The addition of service user identity, friendship group norms, and friendship group identity at step 4 led to a further 10 percent increase in the amount of variance explained (*F change* =2.62 p <.05). In the final regression equation perceived behavioral control and friendship group identity emerged as significant predictors explaining 48 percent of the variance in intentions F (7, 66) = 2.90, p < .01.

Table 3.1
Descriptive Statistics and Intercorrelations

Variable	Mean	SD	2	3	4	5	6	7	8	9	10
2. Behavior	0.61	0.49	—	.27*	.19	.23*	.19	.28*	-.07	.04	-.04
3. Intention	4.55	0.97		—	-.15	.45**	.12	.38**	.00	.24*	.10
4. Subjective norm	3.39	1.98			—	.00	-.03	.02	-.20	.08	.11
5. Perceived behavioral control	4.45	0.93				—	.38**	.34**	.10	.03	.21
6. Attitude	4.37	0.96					—	.19	-.07	-.06	.21
7. Service User Identity	2.84	0.90						—	.14	.37**	.12
8. Friendship Group Identity	2.53	1.37							—	.50**	-.27*
9. Friendship Group Norm	2.33	1.04								—	.21
10. Prior Behavior	1.46	0.50									—

Note. $* p < .05$; $** p < .01$

Table 3.2
Standardized Coefficients from Hierarchical Regression Analysis
Predicting Behavioral Intentions

Predictor	Step 1	Step 2	Step 3	Step 4
Attitude	0.20	0.05	0.04	0.01
Subjective Norm	0.04	0.04	0.03	0.10
Perceived Behavioral Control		0.35**	0.34**	0.33**
Prior Behaviour			0.05	0.00
Service User Identity				0.16
Friendship Group Norms				0.30*
Friendship Group Identity				0.22

Table 3.3
Logistic Regression Analyses Predicting Behavior

Predictor	Step 1	Step 2	Step 3	Step 4	Step 5
Behavioral Intention	2.49**	2.42**	2.41**	2.42**	2.22**
Perceived Behavioral Control		1.21	1.03	1.07	1.17
Attitude			1.40	1.40	1.25
Subjective Norm			1.22	1.22	1.35
Prior Behavior			0.27	0.75	0.49
Service User Identity					2.24*
Friendship Group Norm					0.90
Friendship Group Identity					0.83

Note. * $p < .05$;   ** $p < .01$

Determinants of Behavior

Behavior was coded using a binary scale, so a hierarchical logistic regression analyses was used to test whether TPB and social identity variables predicted participation. Variables were entered in five steps: (1) behavioral intention; (2) perceived behavioral control; (3) attitude and subjective norms; (4) prior behavior; (5) social identity, group norms, and group identity (See table 3.3).

Behavioral intentions accounted for 14 percent of the variance in behavior at step 1, $\chi^2 = 13.53$, $df = 1$, $p < .001$. However, perceived behavioral control, at step two, and attitude and subjective norms, entered at step three, explained an additional 4 percent of the variance in uptake (perceived control: $\chi^2 = 0.32$, $df = 1$, $p =$ n.s; and attitudes and subjective norms: $\chi^2 = 2.56$, $df = 1$, $p =$ n.s., respectively). This pattern was also seen in prior behavior, entered at step four, as it also did not significantly account for any additional variance, $\chi^2 = 0.23$, $df = 1$, $p =$ n.s. However, identity variables (service user identity, group identity and group norms) contributed 5 percent to the overall explained variance in behavior, $\chi^2 = 4.51$, $df = 3$, $p =$ n.s. Although the step was not significant, service user identity emerged as a significant influence on behavior.

In the final regression equation, behavioral intentions and service user identity emerged as significant predictors of housing support use one year after completing the interview. However, attitudes and perceived behavioral control were not significantly related to participants behavior.[1]

Discussion

The present paper tested the applicability of the TPB and variables from social identity theory to predict use of housing support services. The results offer support for the TPB: As predicted, behavioral intention remained a significant predictor of behavior, even when a range of variables from social identity theory were statistically controlled. More importantly, behavioral intentions better predicted behavior than did prior behavior, providing further support for the sufficiency of the TPB (Ajzen, 1991). In contrast with our prior research (see Christian & Abrams, under review; Christian & Armitage, 2002), subjective norm was not directly related to behavior, although service user identity was. The following discussion focuses on the implications for theory and practice.

Theoretical Implications

Ajzen (1991) regards the inclusion of prior behavior within the TPB as a test of its sufficiency. In this respect, the model passed with flying colors: past behavior was not the best predictor of future behavior (see Sutton, 1994). However, in keeping with Ajzen's (1991) argument that the TPB is "...open to the inclusion of additional predictors if it can be shown that they capture a significant proportion of the variance in intention or behavior after the theory's current variables have been taken into account" (p. 199), the present research showed an independent effect of identity on behavior. Interestingly, the effect of identity persisted over the period of a year, implying that people's identities may have been temporally stable. Charng et al. (1988) have shown that, although attitudes and subjective norms are important in initiating behavior, over time, they become less important because people's self-identity concerns come to the fore. In other words, although attitudes, and norms are important determinants of behavior, at some point the need to maintain one's self-concept (e.g., as a blood donor in the case of Charng et al., 1988) outweighs the impact of attitudes and subjective norms. A similar pattern of findings is shown in the present study. Future work might usefully examine the relationship between identity stability and past behavior in order to further understanding between habit and self-identity (cf. Conner, Sheeran, Norman, & Armitage, 2000).

Contrary to what might be predicted by social identity theory, neither friendship group identity nor friendship group norm were predictive of behavior. This raises two possible explanations that are worthy of further research. First, it is possible that normative identification might be with housing support workers and not with friends or others in informal support networks. In other words, there may be a hierarchy of identifications in which support workers are ranked above friends. The second possibility is that friendship groups are less stable than support worker groups and are therefore easier to identify with. It would therefore be interesting to utilize social network analysis to investigate shifts in friendship patterns.

Implications for Homelessness Literature

While interesting, much of the literature on homelessness actually describes initial causes of homelessness, i.e., leaving home, domestic violence, etc. The literature makes no attempt to understand *how* these issues might be internalized, how homelessness is perpetuated, and what may facilitate individuals' efforts to find a home. In particular there is little analysis of the impact of personal and group relationships on individuals' responses to homelessness. The present and related research (see Christian & Abrams, under review; Christian & Armitage, 2002; Christian & Maio, 2001) provides some of the earliest systematic research into these questions, and further insights are likely to be produced from ongoing research into social stigma, attitudes to authority and social rank theory.

Conclusions and Caveats

In conclusion, the present research provides the first concrete step towards looking at the motivations for entering and sustaining participation in housing support programmes. For those who create and monitor such services, it is vital to understand the effects of homeless people's motivations. By assessing homeless people's use of such programmes, this research provides a new avenue for understanding homeless clients' motivations, and can also potentially answer questions about the most effective means for providing assistance. The research found that housing support agencies must pay more attention to homeless people's service user identity and intentions as a means for increasing housing uptake—especially in the long-term.

Note

1.   Additionally, we also explored the moderating impact of service user identity— briefly we tested whether for individuals with high service user identity, attitudes and perceived behavioral control might be stronger predictors of intention, but for individuals with low service user identity, subjective norms might be more relevant. Moderated regression analyses suggest that service user identity moderates the impact of perceived behavioral control on intention, but not on uptake behavior (p's > .05). Also, subsequent analysis shows that there is no moderating effect for service user identity on attitude.

References

Abrams, D., Ando, K., & Hinkle, S. (1998) Psychological attachment to the group: Cross cultural differences in organizational identification and subjective norms as predictors of workers' turnover intentions. *Personality and Social Psychology Bulletin, 10*, 1027-1039.

Abrams, D., & Hogg, M.A. (1990). Social identification, self-categorization and social influence, In M. Hewstone and W. Stroebe (Eds.), *Review of European Social Psychology*, (Vol.1, pp 195-228), Chichester: John Wiley & Sons.

Ajzen, I. (1991). The theory of planned behavior. Special Issue: Theories of cognitive self-regulation. *Organizational Behavior and Human Decision Processes, 50*, 2, 179-211.

Akilu, F. (1992). Multi-method approach to the study of homelessness; P. Kennett (Ed.), *New approaches to homelessness*, (pp. 62-73). Working Paper 104. SAUS Publications.

Anderson, I. (1994). *Access to housing for low income single people: A review of recent research and current policy issues*. The Centre for Housing Policy, University of York, England.

Armitage, C. J., & Conner, M. (2001). Efficacy of the theory of planned behavior: A meta-analytic review. *British Journal of Social Psychology, 40*, 471-499.

Belcher, J., & Di Blasio, F. (1990). *Helping the homeless: Where do we go from here?* Lexington: MA: Lexington Books.

Bates, D.S., & Toro, P.A. (1999). Developing measures to assess social support amongst homeless and poor people. *Journal of Community Psychology, 27*, 137-156.

Burrows, R. (1997). The social distribution of the experience of homelessness. In R. Burrows, N. Pleace & D. Quilgars (Eds.), *Homelessness and social policy*, (pp. 50-68). London: Routledge.

Charng, H.W., Piliavin, J.A., & Callero, P.L. (1988). Role identity and reasoned action in the prediction of repeated behaviour. *Social Psychology Quarterly, 51*, 303-215.

Christian, J., & Abrams, D. (under review). The effects of social identification, norms and attitudes on use of outreach services by homeless people. *Social Psychology Quarterly*.

Christian, J., & Armitage, C.J. (2002). Attitudes and intentions of homeless persons towards service provision in South Wales. *British Journal of Social Psychology*, 41, 219-231.

Christian, J., & Maio, G.R. Homeless people's housing uptake: The neglected role of self-fulfilment. Housing Studies Association Conference, Cardiff, 4-5 Sept. 2001.

Conner, M., Sheeran, P., Norman, P., & Armitage, C. J. (2000). Temporal stability as a moderator of relationships in the theory of planned behaviour. *British Journal of Social Psychology, 39*, 469-493.

Farrington, A., & Robinson, W.P. (1999). Homelessness and strategies of identity maintenance: A participant observation study. *Journal of Community and Applied Social Psychology, 9*, 175-194.

Fitzpatrick, S. Kemp, P., & Klinker, S. (2000). *Single homelessness: An overview of research in Britain,* York: Joseph Rowntree Foundation.

Jahiel, R.I. (1992). Services for homeless people: An overview. In R.I. Jahiel (Ed.), *Homelessness: A prevention orientated approach*, pp. 167-192. Baltimore, MD: Johns Hopkins University Press.

Jetten, J., Postmes, T., & McAuliffe, B. (2002). 'We're all individuals': Group norms of individualism and collectivism, levels of identification and identity threat. *European Journal of Social Psychology, 32*, 189-207.

Milburn, N.G., Watt, R.J. & Anderson, S.L. (1986). *Analysis of current research methods for studying the homeless.* Washington, DC: Howard University Press.

O'Callaghan, B. Dominian, L., Evans, A., Dix, J., Smith, R., Williams, P., & Zimmeck, M. (1996). *Study of homeless applicants*. London: DETR Publications.

Pleace, N. (1998). Single homelessness as social exclusion: the unique and the extreme. *Social Policy and Administration, 32*, 46- 59.

Randall, G. & Brown, S. (1996). *From street to home: An evaluation of phase two of the rough sleepers' initiative*. Norwich: HMSO Department of the Environment.

Social Trends (2001). London: HMSO.

Shelter (2001). Shelter Fact Sheet. London: Shelter.

Snow, D.A., & Anderson, L. (1987). Identity work among the homeless: The verbal construction and avowal of personal identities. *American Journal of Sociology, 92,* 1336-1371.

Sutton, S. (1994). The past predicts the future: Interpreting behaviour-behaviour relationships in social psychological models of health behaviour. In D. R. Rutter & L. Quine (Eds.), *Social psychology and health: European perspectives* (pp. 71-88). Aldershot, UK: Avebury.

Tajfel, H. & Turner, J.C. (1979). An integrative theory of intergroup conflict. In W.G. Austin & S. Worchel (Eds.), *The social psychology of intergroup relations*, (pp.33-47). Monterey, CA: Brooks-Cole.

Terry, D.J., Hogg, M.A., & White, K.M. (1999). The theory of planned behaviours: Self-identity, social identity, and group norms. *British Journal of Social* Psychology, *38,* 225-244.

Toro, P. A., & Wall, D. D. (1991). Research on homeless persons: Diagnostic comparisons and practice implications. *Professional Psychology: Research and Practice, 22,* 479-488.

Wilcox, S. (2000). *Housing Finance Review.* York: Joseph Rowntree Foundation.

Wright, B.R.E. (1998). Behavioral intentions and opportunities among homeless individuals: A reinterpretation of the theory of reasoned action. *Social Psychology Quarterly, 61,* 271-286.

4

Descriptive Norms as an Additional Predictor in the Theory of Planned Behavior: A Meta-Analysis

Amanda Rivis and Paschal Sheeran

The theory of planned behavior (TPB; Ajzen, 1991) is perhaps the most influential theory for the prediction of social and health behaviors. This model is an extension of the theory of reasoned action (TRA; Ajzen & Fishbein, 1980) and incorporates both social influences and personal factors as predictors. Social influences are conceptualised in terms of the pressure that people perceive from important others to perform, or not to perform, a behavior (*subjective norm*). Subjective norm is determined by beliefs about the extent to which important others want them to perform a behavior (*normative beliefs*, e.g., "My friends think that I should engage in a binge drinking session") multiplied by one's *motivation to comply* with those people's views (e.g., "I generally want to do what my friends think I should do"). Subjective norms are proposed to influence behavior through their impact upon *intentions*, (e.g., "I intend to engage in a binge drinking session"). Intentions summarise a person's motivation to act in a particular manner and indicate how hard the person is willing to try and how much time and effort s/he is willing to devote in order to perform a behavior. Also important in the prediction of intentions are people's positive or negative evaluations of their performing a behavior (*attitudes*, e.g., "For me, engaging in a binge drinking session would be wise/foolish") and the degree of control that they believe they have over performing the behavior (*perceived behavioral control*, e.g., "Engaging in a binge drinking session is entirely under/outside my control"). Like subjective norms,

Author Note: We thank Katy White and Simon Cooper for providing additional data and information.

43

attitudes and perceived behavioral control are determined by certain beliefs. Underlying attitudes are beliefs about the consequences of performing the behavior multiplied by evaluations of those consequences (*behavioral beliefs*, e.g., It is likely/unlikely that I will miss lectures if I engage in a binge drinking session" and *outcome evaluations*, e.g., "Missing lectures would be good/bad"); underlying perceived behavioral control are beliefs concerning factors that inhibit or facilitate performance of the behavior multiplied by the perceived power of these factors (*control beliefs*, e.g., "Engaging in a binge drinking session requires a lot of money" and *power*, e.g., "Having a lot of money increases the likelihood of my engaging in a binge drinking session"). According to the TPB, the more positive people's attitudes and subjective norms, and the greater their perceived behavioral control regarding a behavior, the more likely people are to intend to perform that behavior. Similarly, the stronger people's intentions, the more likely they are to perform the behavior.

The TPB has been successfully applied to a wide range of behaviors and meta-analytic reviews support the theory's predictions. For example, intentions typically explain between 19 percent and 38 percent of the variance in behavior in prospective studies (Ajzen, 1991; Armitage & Conner, 2001; Sheeran, 2002; Sheeran & Orbell, 1998). Attitudes and subjective norms (i.e., the theory of reasoned action) account for 33 percent to 50 percent of the variance in intentions (Ajzen, 1991; Armitage & Conner, 2001; Sheeran & Taylor, 1997). The addition of perceived behavioral control typically increases the explained variance in intentions by 5 percent—12 percent (Ajzen, 1991; Armitage & Conner, 2001; Conner & Armitage, 1998; Sheeran & Taylor, 1997) and increases the variance explained in behavior by 2—12 percent over and above intentions (Armitage & Conner, 2001; Godin & Kok, 1996). Although these effect sizes are impressive (cf. Cohen, 1992), it is also apparent that the TPB leaves a substantial proportion of the variance in intentions and behavior to be explained. While some of the unexplained variance can be attributed to methodological factors (cf. Sutton, 1998), conceptual factors should also be considered.

The comparative weakness of the subjective norm-intention relation is of particular relevance here. Armitage and Conner's (2001) meta-analysis showed that the subjective norm-intention correlation is significantly weaker than the attitude-intention and perceived behavioral control-intention relationships. It has been argued that the lack of association between subjective norms and intentions indicates that intentions are influenced primarily by personal factors (attitude and perceived behavioral control; Ajzen, 1991). However, other evidence suggests that the narrow conceptualisation of the normative component in the TPB may be responsible for the attenuation of the subjective norm-intention relation (cf. Armitage & Conner, 2001; Sheeran & Orbell, 1999).

There is an important distinction in the literature on social influence between injunctive norms (i.e., what significant others think the person *ought* to do) and descriptive norms (i.e., what significant others themselves *do*) because these are separate sources of motivation (Deutsch & Gerard, 1955). The subjective norm component of the TPB is an injunctive social norm because it is concerned with perceived social pressure, that is, the person's potential to gain approval or suffer sanctions from significant others for engaging in a behavior. Descriptive norms, on the other hand, refer to perceptions of significant others' *own* attitudes and behaviors in the domain.[1] Here, the opinions and actions of significant others provide information that people may use in deciding what to do themselves (e.g., "If everyone's doing it, then it must be a sensible thing to do" cf. Cialdini, Kallgren & Reno, 1991).

Although the discriminant and convergent validity of the descriptive norm and subjective norm constructs has been supported by factor analysis (e.g., Grube et al., 1986; Sheeran & Orbell, 1999; White, Terry, & Hogg, 1994), it remains unclear how well descriptive norms predict intentions. Three lines of evidence support this view. First, some studies have reported medium to strong correlations between descriptive norms and intentions whereas other studies have found weak or non-significant relationships. For example, Rivis and Sheeran (2001a, Study 2) obtained a correlation of .70 between descriptive norms and intentions in relation to young people's binge drinking behavior, whereas Stanton et al. (1996) obtained a correlation of only .04 in relation to condom use. Second, findings have been contradictory when descriptive norm has been simultaneously entered in the regression equation alongside attitudes, subjective norms and perceived behavioral control. For example, Conner, Martin, Silverdale and Grogan (1996) found that perceptions of others' behavior contributed to the prediction of intentions to diet, but Astrom & Rise (2001), in a very similar domain (healthy eating), found that group norms predicted adults' intentions *only* among those who identified strongly with the salient reference group. Third, studies that examined whether descriptive norms predict intentions *after* controlling for the effects of the attitudes, subjective norms and perceived behavioral control have also produced conflicting findings. For example, Sheeran and Orbell (1999, Studies 1 & 2) found that descriptive norms captured a significant proportion of the variance in intentions to play the lottery after taking TPB predictors into account. Conversely, Povey, Conner, Sparks, James and Shepherd (2000) found that descriptive norms did not significantly contribute to the prediction of intentions to eat healthily.

Another difficulty is that several studies that controlled for the TPB predictors included other "additional" predictors in the same step of the regression as descriptive norms but did not report the squared semi-partial correlation coefficients to indicate the unique variance accounted for by descriptive norms (see Conner & McMillan, 1999, for an exception). For example, Sheeran and Orbell (1999) showed that the increments of 11 percent and 26 percent in the variance in intentions were accounted for by descriptive norms and anticipated regret (in Studies 1 & 2, respectively). However, it is unclear what proportion of these increases in variance were attributable to descriptive norms.

Thus, the aims of the present study are to quantify the strength of the descriptive norm-intention relation and to determine whether descriptive norms enhance the variance explained in intentions after TPB predictors have been taken into account using meta-analytical procedures. An additional aim is to examine two potential moderators of the descriptive norm-intention relation: age and type of health behavior. Moderator analyses could prove useful in explaining why some studies obtained strong descriptive-norm relations whereas other studies found only weak relationships.

Research indicates that adolescence is associated with heightened sensitivity to social influences (Suls & Mullen, 1982; Pasupathi, 1999). A key life task during adolescence is establishing one's identity (Erikson, 1950; 1968) and this process is aided by seeking information and guidance from peers (Sebald, 1989). Because observing the behavior of others is one way that information about the *norm*al way to behave can be obtained, perceptions of others' behavior may be particularly influential in motivating behavior among adolescents. Indeed, several researchers have argued that social influences from peers are the most important predictors of behavior among this population (Kandel, 1980; Oetting & Beauvais, 1986, 1987). We therefore predicted that the descriptive norm-intention relation would be significantly stronger among younger samples compared to older samples.

The literature on social influence also suggests that descriptive norms may be more important in motivating decisions to engage in health-risk behaviors than health-promoting behaviors. For example, research on health-related possible selves suggests that health-risk images are more salient than are health-promoting images (Hooker & Kaus, 1994). Health-risk behaviors are also arguably more exciting and enjoyable than health-promoting behaviors. Consequently, people may be more likely to imitate health-risk behaviors such as smoking and drinking than to imitate health-promoting behaviors such as exercise. In sum, there are reasons to anticipate a stronger descriptive norm-intention relationship for health-risk behaviors than for health-promoting behaviors.

The Present Study

The present study uses meta-analysis: (a) to quantify the relationship between descriptive norms and intentions, (b) to assess the predictive validity of descriptive norms after TPB predictors have been taken into account, and (c) to examine age and type of health behavior (health-risk versus health-promoting) as potential moderators of the relationship between descriptive norms and intentions.

Method

Sample of Studies

Several methods were used to generate the sample of studies: (a) computerised searches of social scientific databases (PsychLit, Web of Science, Index to Theses, Conference Papers Index), (b) reference lists in each article identified above were evaluated for inclusion, and (c) the authors of published articles were contacted and requests were made for unpublished studies and studies in press.

There was one inclusion criterion for the review: a bivariate statistical relationship between intention and descriptive norms had to be retrievable from studies. Using this criterion, a total of eighteen articles comprising twenty-one tests of the relationship between intentions and descriptive norms could be included.

Study Characteristics

Table 4.1 presents the characteristics and effect sizes obtained from each test of the descriptive norm-intention relation. Fourteen hypotheses involved applications of the TPB in the context of descriptive norms. Sixteen hypotheses came from younger samples (i.e., school children and undergraduate students) and five came from older, non-student, samples. Sixteen studies examined descriptive norms in relation to a health-related behavior.

Meta-analytic Strategy

The effect size estimate employed here was the weighted average of the sample correlations, r_+. r_+ describes the direction and strength of the relationship between two variables with a range of -1.0 to $+1.0$. Computing the weighted average effect size requires a transformation of the correlation from each relevant hypothesis into Fisher's Z. The following formula is then employed:

$$\text{Average } Z \text{ value} = \frac{\Sigma(N_i \underline{x} \, r \, zi)}{\Sigma(N_i)}$$

where r_{zi} = the Fisher's Z transformation of the correlation from each study i,

N_i = number of participants in study i.

In this way correlations based on larger samples receive greater weight than those from smaller samples. The average Z value is then backtransformed to give r_+ (see Hedges & Olkin, 1985; Hunter, Schmidt, & Jackson, 1982).

Homogeneity analyses were conducted using the Chi-square statistic (Hunter et al., 1982) to determine whether variation among the correlations was greater than chance. The degrees of freedom for the Chi-square test is $k - 1$, where k is the number of independent correlations. If Chi-square is non-significant, then the correlations are homogenous and the average weighted effect size, r_+, can be said to represent the population effect size.

Computation of weighted average effect size and homogeneity statistics were conducted using Schwarzer's (1988) *Meta* computer program.

Table 4.1

Studies of the Relationship between Descriptive Norms and Behavioral Intention

Author(s)	Sample	Behavior	N	r
Astrom & Rise (2001)	Random sample of 25 year olds	Healthy eating	709	32
Berg, Jonsson & Conner (2000)	School pupils (11, 13 and 15 year olds)	Milk and bread choice	1584	.50
Buunk & Bakker (1995, Study 1)	White Dutch adults (mean age = 35 years)	Extradyadic sex	250	.57
Buunk & Bakker (1995, Study 2)	17 to 65 year olds (mean age = 35 years)	Extradyadic sex	250	.48
Buunk, Bakker, Siero, van den Eijnden Yzer (1998)	Adult females and males (18-70 years)	Condom use	711	.47
Conner, Martin, Silverdale & Grogan (1996)	Convenience sample of early-adolescent and pre-adolescent boys and girls	Dieting	231	.41
Conner & McMillan (1999)	Male and female undergraduates	Cannabis use	249	.56
Cooper & Donald (2001)	Undergraduate students	Cannabis and ecstasy use	130	.62
Grube, Morgan & McGree (1986, Study 1)	Primary school children	Cigarette smoking	752	.29
Grube, Morgan & McGree (1986, Study 2)	College students	Cigarette smoking	147	.22
McMillan & Conner (2001)	Undergraduate students	Illicit drug use	494	.62

Table 4.1 (cont.)

Author(s)	Sample	Behavior	N	r
Povey , Conner, Sparks, James, & Shepherd (2000)	Newspaper ad respondents (median age = 38 years)	Healthy eating	242	.21
Rivis & Sheeran (2001a, Study 1; 2001b)[a]	Undergraduate students	Binge drinking and physical exercise	333	.52
Rivis & Sheeran (2001a, Study 2)	Undergraduate students	Binge drinking	183	.70
Schaalma, Kok, & Peters (1993)	Random sample of Dutch secondary school pupils (12-19 years)	Condom use	1018	.34
Sheeran & Orbell (1999, Study 1)	Random sample of the public in a UK city	Lottery play	200	.44
Sheeran & Orbell (1999, Study 2)	Undergraduate students	Lottery play	111	.51
Sheeran & Orbell (1999, Study 3)	Undergraduate students	Lottery play	115	.46
Stanton, Li, Black, Ricardo, Galbraith, Feigelman, & Kaljee (1996)	African American young people living in urban public housing (9-15 years)	Condom use	44	.04
Terry & Hogg (1996, Study 1)	University students	Physical exercise	133	.23
White, Terry & Hogg (1994)	Undergraduate students	Condom use	211	.56

Note. [a] The same two samples but different health behaviors were studied

Multiple Behaviors and Multiple Measures

Where studies included more than one behavior and reported separate bivariate associations for each behavior (e.g., cannabis use and ecstasy use; Cooper & Donald, 2001), then the weighted average correlation of the behaviors within that study was used as the unit of analysis. Similarly, where studies included more than one measure of descriptive norms (e.g., peer smoking and parental smoking; Grube et al., 1986), the weighted average correlation within that study was used as the unit of analysis. This procedure avoids violation of the independence assumption that underlies the validity of meta-analytic procedures.

Results

Cohen (1992) provides useful guidelines for interpreting the size of sample-weighted average correlations (r_+). According to Cohen, $r_+ = .10$ is small, $r_+ = .30$ is medium, and $r_+ = .50$ is large. We use these qualitative indices to interpret our findings.

The Overall Descriptive Norm-Intention Relationship

Across all studies ($k = 21$, $N = 8097$), a large positive sample size-weighted average correlation between descriptive norms and intention was obtained ($r_+ = .44$). The average r_+ was highly significant and had a narrow 95 percent confidence interval (95 percent CI = .43–.46). To determine the robustness of this correlation, we estimated the number of unpublished studies containing null results which would be required to invalidate this study's conclusion that intentions and descriptive norms are significantly related ($p < .05$). The 'Fail-Safe N' (Rosenthal, 1984) was 166. Since this exceeds the recommended tolerance level of $5k + 10$, the average correlation obtained here can be viewed as robust. The homogeneity statistic shows considerable variation in the correlations reported in previous studies ($\chi^2 = 213.35$, $p < .001$) which encourages a search for moderators.

Descriptive Norms in the Context of the TPB

In order to examine the strength of the sample size weighted average correlation between descriptive norms and intentions in the context of the TPB, we conducted a meta-analysis of those studies that included intercorrelations between all TPB variables and descriptive norms ($k = 14$, $N = 5810$). Table 4.2 shows that when only those studies that reported all relevant correlations are included in the analysis, the sample-weighted average correlation between descriptive norms and intention was almost identical to that obtained previously ($r_+ = .46$ versus $r_+ = .44$). The sample-weighted average correlation between subjective norms and descriptive norms was only .38, which indicates that there is only modest conceptual overlap between these constructs. Interestingly, descriptive norms had a similar correlation with attitude ($r_+ = .38$), but a small average r with perceived behavioral control ($r_+ = .08$).

Table 4.2
Meta-Analysis of Descriptive Norms and the TPB (N = 5810: k = 14).

Relationship	r_+	95 percent CI	Chi-square
Intention-Attitude	.58	.56–.60	138.54***
Intention-Subjective Norm	.44	.42–.46	87.21***
Intention-Perceived Behavioral Control	.21	.19–.24	1022.84***
Intention-Descriptive Norms	.46	.44–.48	144.46***
Attitude-Subjective Norms	.44	.42–.46	119.03***
Attitude-Perceived Behavioral Control	.16	.14–.19	423.68***
Attitude-Descriptive Norms	.38	.36–.41	66.46***
Subjective Norms-Perceived Behavioral Control	.09	.06–.11	323.46***
Subjective Norms-Descriptive Norms	.38	.36–.40	93.01***
Perceived Behavioral Control-Descriptive Norms	.08	.06–.11	328.79***

Note. N = Sample size upon which sample-weighted average correlation is based; k = Number of correlations; r_+ = Sample-weighted average correlation between predictor variables; CI = Confidence interval; Chi-square = Chi-square test for homogeneity of sample correlations.
*** $p < .001$.

In order to examine the extent to which descriptive norms enhance the prediction of intention after TPB variables have been statistically controlled, we conducted a two-step hierarchical regression using the average correlations as the input matrix. Attitudes, subjective norms, and perceived behavioral control entered the equation at the first step, and descriptive norms entered at the second step. Table 4.3 shows that all TPB variables had significant beta coefficients in the first equation and accounted for 39 percent of the variance in intentions. Importantly, however, the addition of descriptive norms led to a significant increment in the variance explained in intentions (R^2 change = .05, F change = 461.51, p < .001). In the final equation, 44 percent of the variance was accounted for and significant betas were obtained for all variables. Interestingly, the beta for descriptive norms was higher than the betas for subjective norms and perceived behavioral control, and was surpassed only by attitudes.

Table 4.3
Hierarchical Regression of Intention on the TPB and Descriptive Norms
(N = 5810)

Step	Variables Entered	Beta	Beta
1.	Attitude	.46***	.40***
	Subjective Norms	.23***	.16***
	Perceived Control	.12***	.11***
2.	Descriptive Norms	-	.24***
R^2		.39	.44
Model F		1246.70***	1124.57***

*** p <.001.

Moderators of the Descriptive Norm-Intention Relationship

Both moderators were treated as categorical variables in order to test moderation. We computed the effect size for two levels of the moderator and used Fisher's Z test for the comparison of independent correlations to test the significance of the difference between effect sizes. Table 4.4 presents separate effect sizes for younger samples (i.e., children and students) versus older samples, and health-risk versus health-promoting behaviors.[2]

Table 4.4
Meta-Analyses of Age and Type of Health Behavior as Moderators of the Descriptive Norm-Intention Relation

Moderator	k	N	r_+	95 percent CI	Chi-square
Younger samples	16	5935	.46	.44–.48	170.91***
Older samples	5	2162	.41	.37–.44	39.97***
Health risk behavior	6	1955	.48	.45–.51	113.04***
Health-promoting behavior	7	3068	.37	.33–.40	43.01***

Note. k = Number of correlations; N = Sample size upon which sample-weighted average correlation is based; CI = Confidence interval; Chi-square = Chi-square test for homogeneity of sample correlations.
*** $p < .001$.

Sample age. We hypothesised that there would be a stronger correlation between descriptive norms and intention for younger samples than for older samples. Consistent with our prediction, the effect size for children and students ($r_+ = .46$) was significantly larger than the effect size for older samples ($r_+ = .41$), $Z = 2.45$, $p < .01$. Thus, the intentions of children and students are more strongly associated with their perceptions of others' behavior than are the intentions of older samples.

Health behavior. Consistent with our second moderator hypothesis, health-risk behaviors had significantly stronger descriptive norm-intention relations than health-promoting behaviors. The average correlation for health-risk behaviors ($r_+ = .48$) was significantly larger than the correlation for health-promoting behaviors (r_+ = .37), Z = 4.65, p < .001. Perceptions of other people's behavior is a better predictor of intentions to engage in health-risk behaviors compared to intentions to engage in health-promoting behaviors.

Discussion

This is the first study to quantify the relationship between descriptive norms and intentions using meta-analytic procedures. A large sample size-weighted average correlation was obtained between descriptive norms and intentions across all studies (r_+ = .44, k = 21, N = 8097) and in the context of the TPB (r_+ = .46, k = 14, N = 5810). A regression analysis showed that TPB variables explained 39 percent of the variance in intentions–the identical proportion of variance obtained in Armitage and Conner's (2001) meta-analysis of the TPB. Importantly, descriptive norms significantly increased the variance in intentions, contributing a further 5 percent over and above the TPB predictors.

The predictive success of descriptive norms in the context of the TPB has considerable theoretical value. Several authors have suggested that the descriptive norm construct may qualify as an additional predictor in the TPB (e.g., Sheeran & Orbell, 1999), although until now this variable has only been investigated in relation to single behaviors and among relatively small sample sizes. In addition, most of these studies failed to control for the effects of the TPB variables, or did not indicate what proportion of the increment in variance was uniquely attributable to descriptive norms. Hence, the utility of descriptive norms in the TPB remained unclear. However, the results of our analyses based upon 14 TPB studies involving a total sample size of N = 5810, and covering a wide range of behavioral domains, provides strong evidence in support of the predictive validity of descriptive norms. The consideration that descriptive norms contributed an additional 5 percent to the variance in intention after attitudes, subjective norms, and perceived behavioral control have been taken into account suggests that the descriptive norm construct warrants inclusion in the model (cf. Ajzen, 1991).

Three sets of results attest to the validity of our findings. First, the average correlation between descriptive norms and intentions across all studies was almost identical to that obtained in our analysis of the TPB studies only. It is unlikely, therefore, that TPB studies are biased against finding stronger descriptive norm-intention correlations compared to non-TPB studies. Second, the modest correlation between descriptive norms and subjective norms (.38) adds to the evidence supporting the discriminant and convergent validity of the two constructs (see Grube et al., 1986; Sheeran and Orbell, 1999; White et al.,1994): descriptive norms and subjective norms do appear to be conceptually distinct. Third, the proportion of the variance in intentions explained by TPB variables was identical to that reported in Armitage and Conner's (2001) extensive review of the TPB. This suggests that the studies included in this review are representative. In sum, there are good reasons to believe that the findings obtained here are valid.

In addition to assessing the strength of the descriptive norm-intention relation, we also examined two potential moderators of this relationship, namely, age and type of health behavior. In relation to age, we hypothesised that the descriptive norm-intention relationship would be stronger among younger samples. This prediction was based on research suggesting that children and young adults are more susceptible to social influence than older adults because of young people's need to establish their self identity (Erikson, 1950; 1968). Meta-analysis supported our prediction. This finding is consistent with evidence from life span developmental psychology, which indicates that adolescents and young adults are particularly sensitive to the conformity pressures associated with real, and perceived, social norms (Suls & Mullen, 1982; Pasupathi, 1999). This is perhaps unsurprising given that the school/college years are likely to afford the greatest contact with peers. As a result of transition from junior to senior school, and then to college or university, young people are frequently faced with the challenge of establishing new friendships. Imitating the behavior of peers may therefore be an attempt to gain group acceptance (Castro, Maddahian, Newcomb, & Bentler, 1987; Eiser & van der Pligt, 1984) and achieve categorisation as a group member (i.e. group identification) (cf. Terry, Hogg & White, 1999), which are strong needs among adolescents. This suggests that the descriptive norm-intention relation should be weaker among people who do not wish to define themselves in terms of the group norm. Consistent with this reasoning, two of the studies included in this current review found that the relationship between group norms and intention is stronger for individuals who identify with a behaviorally relevant reference group (cf. Astrom & Rise, 2001; Terry & Hogg, 1996). However, because small sample sizes precluded meaningful comparisons of strong versus weak identifiers, the generality of this finding is unclear. Thus, future research might systematically explore the relationship between group identification, descriptive norms and intentions in relation to a wide range of behaviors to enable more definitive conclusions to be reached.

We also hypothesised that the descriptive norm-intention relationship would be stronger for health-risk behaviors than for health-promoting behaviors. This prediction was informed by research on health-images which suggests that health-risk behaviors are more salient than health-promoting behaviors, and our own reasoning that health-risk behaviors are more enjoyable than health-promoting behaviors. Meta-analytic findings supported our hypothesis. While further research is required to examine possible explanations for this moderating effect, evidence from a variety of sources is consistent with our "salience" and "enjoyment" hypotheses. Research on social images suggests that health-risk, or negative, images are more vivid than health-promoting, or positive, images. For example, Blanton et al. (2001) demonstrated that behavioral decisions related to condom use are influenced by people's images of the type of person who does *not* use condoms, but not by people's images of the type of person who *does* use condoms. In addition, when asked to describe their feared (i.e., negative) future selves and their hoped-for (positive) future selves, people tend to generate a greater number of self-images relating to the former (Hooker & Kaus, 1994). Finally, research on cognitive versus affective components of attitudes has shown that smoking decisions are driven more by "enjoyment" than by "health" considerations (Trafimow & Sheeran, 1998). Notwithstanding this evidence in support of the greater salience and enjoyment of health-risk behaviors as explanations for our finding here, future research might also explore other potential moderators of the descriptive norm-intention relationship. For example, research has demonstrated that the importance of social influences depends not only upon the type of behavior (e.g., whether it is primarily a "private" or a "public" behavior), but also upon the type of person (e.g., whether their intentions are primarily under "attitudinal" control or "normative" control) (Trafimow & Finlay, 1996).

Although the present findings suggest that descriptive norms are an important factor in motivating behavioral decisions, the correlational data upon which our analyses are based preclude causal inferences. Thus, the data do not indicate whether perceptions of other people's behavior direct behavioral intentions or vice versa. For example, research by Farrell and Danish (1993) indicates that the significant association between descriptive norms and intentions may be the result of selection processes rather than social influence processes. According to this explanation, a person chooses his or her friends on the basis of similar attitudes and lifestyle practices. A strong version of the selection hypothesis would suggest that attitudes determine descriptive norm estimates. If this was accurate, we would have expected a large correlation between attitudes and descriptive norms, and descriptive norms to be non-significant in the regression of intentions on the TPB and descriptive norm. However, the correlation obtained here between attitudes and descriptive norms was not "large" according to Cohen's (1992) criteria and descriptive norms were a significant predictor in the regression. Indeed, contrary to the selection hypothesis, experimental research by Cialdini and colleagues suggests that descriptive norms have a causal impact on criterion variables. For example, Cialdini, Kallgren and Reno (1991) showed that manipulating peoples' focus on the descriptive norm for littering significantly affected subsequent littering behavior. Clearly, further experimental research on behaviors such as those included in this review is needed to glean more conclusive evidence concerning the direction of effects for descriptive norms.

Finally, our findings have a number of implications for interventions aimed at reducing the prevalence of health-risk behaviors and increasing health-enhancing behaviors. The fact that descriptive norms had a larger regression coefficient in the prediction of intention than did subjective norm suggests that observing the behavior of others may be of greater importance in health-related decision making than social pressure from others, particularly in the case of health-risk behaviors. Thus, organising groups in such a manner that people who are *not* performing behaviors such as drug use and binge drinking are in the majority may be beneficial in promoting healthy intentions (cf. Trafimow, 1994). The finding that young people are particularly susceptible to descriptive norms, as indicated by moderator analysis, suggests that interventions should be tailored to the unique needs of adolescents. For example, helping young people to develop a sense of uniqueness (Snyder & Fromkin, 1980) or the use of peers as role models for reducing health-risk behaviors (cf. Cottler et al., 1999), could be particularly effective.

In conclusion, Ajzen (1991) explicitly welcomed research which addresses the role of additional variables in the TPB, stating that:

> The theory of planned behavior is, in principle, open to the inclusion of additional predictors if it can be shown that they capture a significant proportion of the variance in intention or behavior after the theory's current variables have been taken into account. (p. 199).

The findings from the current review satisfy this criterion and provide the best evidence to date to support the inclusion of descriptive norms as an additional predictor in the TPB. To summarise, this review found a medium to strong average correlation between descriptive norms and intention and, more importantly, showed a significant improvement in the predictive validity of the TPB when descriptive norm was included as an additional predictor. Younger samples and health-risk behaviors (rather than health-promoting behaviors) were both associated with stronger correlations between descriptive norms and intention. Our review also indicates that further research is needed in order to identify sociocontextual and dispositional factors that may enhance the strength of the descriptive norm-intention relation, and to clarify the direction of effects for descriptive norms.

Notes

1. Descriptive norms have also been termed "group norms" (e.g., White, Terry, & Hogg, 1994) and "behavioral norms" (e.g., Grube, Morgan & McGree, 1986).
2. Four studies were excluded from the moderator analysis of type of health behavior: The correlations between descriptive norms and intention in Rivis and Sheeran (2001a, Study 1; 2001b) and Berg, et al., (2000) are averaged across health-risk and health-promoting behaviors (see Table 1). Disaggregating the behaviors for moderator analysis would have violated the independence assumption underlying the validity of meta-analysis; Conner et al., (1996) examined dieting, a health behavior which can be categorised as either a health-risk or a health-promoting behavior. This study was also therefore excluded from the analysis.

References

References marked with an asterisk indicate studies included in the meta-analysis.

Ajzen, I. (1991). The theory of planned behavior. *Organizational Behavior and Human Decision Processes, 50*, 179-211.

Ajzen, I., & Fishbein, M. (1980). *Understanding attitudes and predicting social behavior.* Englewood Cliffs, NJ: Prentice-Hall.

Armitage, C. J., & Conner, M. (1999). The theory of planned behaviour: Assessment of predictive validity and "perceived control." *British Journal of Social Psychology, 38*, 35-54.

Armitage, C. J., & Conner, M. (2001). Efficacy of the theory of planned behaviour: A meta-analytic review. *British Journal of Social Psychology, 40*, 471-499.

*Astrom, A. N., & Rise, J. (2001). Young adults' intention to eat healthy food: Extending the theory of planned behaviour. *Psychology and Health, 16*, 223-237.

*Berg, C., Jonsson, I., & Conner, M. (2000). Understanding choice of milk and bread for breakfast among Swedish children aged 11-15 years: An application of the theory of planned behaviour. *Appetite, 34*, 5-19.

Blanton, H., VandenEijnden, R. J. J. M., Buunk, B. P., Gibbons, F. X., Gerrard, M., & Bakker, A. (2001). Accentuate the negative: Social images in the prediction and promotion of condom use. *Journal of Applied Social Psychology, 31*, 274-295.

*Buunk, B. P., & Bakker, A. B. (1995). Extradyadic sex: The role of descriptive and injunctive norms. *The Journal of Sex Research, 32*, 313-318.

*Buunk, B. P., Bakker, A. B., Siero, F. W., VandenEijnden, R. J. J. M., & Yzer, M. C. (1998). Predictors of AIDS-preventive behavioral intentions among adult heterosexuals at risk for HIV-infection: Extending current models and measures. *AIDS Education and Prevention, 10*, 149-172.

Castro, F. G., Maddahian, E., Newcomb, M. D., & Bentler, P. M. (1987). A multivariate model of the determinants of cigarette smoking among adolescents. *Journal of Health and Social Behaviour, 28*, 273-289.

Cohen, J. (1992). A power primer. *Psychological Bulletin, 112*, 155-159.

Conner, M., & Armitage, C. J. (1998). Extending the theory of planned behaviour: A review and avenues for future research. *Journal of Applied Social Psycholgy, 28*, 1429-1464.

*Conner, M., Martin, E., Silverdale, N., & Grogan, S. (1996). Dieting in adolescence: An application of the theory of planned behaviour. *British Journal of Health Psychology, 1*, 315-325.

*Conner, M., & McMillan, B. (1999). Interaction effects in the theory of planned behaviour: Studying cannabis use. *British Journal of Social Psychology, 38*, 195-222.

*Cooper, S., & Donald, I. (2001). Extending the theory of planned behaviour: Roles for descriptive and moral norms. *Paper presented at the British Psychological Society Centenary Conference, Glasgow, March.*

Cottler, L. B., Compton, W. M., Ben Abdallah, A., Cunningham-Williams, R., Abram, F., Fichtenbaum, C., & Dotson, W. (1999). Peer delivered interventions reduce HIV risk behaviors among out-of-treatment drug abusers. *Public Health, 113*, 31-41.

Deutsch, M., & Gerard, H. B. (1955). A study of normative and informational influences upon individual judgement. *Journal of Abnormal and Social Psychology, 51*, 629-636.

Eiser, J. R., & van der Pligt, J. (1984). Attitudinal and social factors in adolescent smoking: In search of peer group influence. *Journal of Applied Social Psychology, 14*, 348-363.

Erikson, E. H. (1950). *Childhood and society.* New York: Norton.

Erikson, E. H. (1968). *Identity: Youth and crisis.* New York: Norton.

Godin, G., & Kok, G. (1996). The theory of planned behavior: A review of its applications to health-related behaviors. *American Journal of Health Promotion, 11*, 87-98.

*Grube, J. W., Morgan, M., & McGree, S. T. (1986). Attitudes and normative beliefs as predictors of smoking intentions and behaviours: A test of three models. *British Journal of Social Psychology, 25*, 81-93.

Hedges, L. V., & Olkin, I. (1985). *Statistical methods for meta-analysis.* New York: Academic Press.

Hooker, K., & Kaus, C. R. (1994). Health-related possible selves in young and middle adulthood. *Psychology and Aging, 9*, 126-133.

Hunter, J. E., Schmidt, F. L., & Jackson, G. B. (1982). *Meta-analysis: Correcting error and bias in research findings.* Newbury Park, CA: Sage.

Kandel, D. B. (1980). Drug and drinking behavior among youth. *Annual Review of Sociology, 6*, 235-285.

Marks, G., & Miller, N. (1987). Ten years of research on the false-consensus effect: An empirical and theoretical review. *Psychological Bulletin, 102*, 72-90.

McMillan, B., & Conner, M. (2001). Applying an extended version of the theory of planned behaviour to illicit drug use among students (manuscript under review).

Oetting, E. R., & Beauvais, F. (1986). Peer cluster theory: Drugs and the adolescent. *Journal of Counseling and Development, 65*, 17-22.

Oetting, E. R., & Beauvais, F. (1987). Common elements in youth drug abuse: Peer clusters and other psychosocial factors. *Journal of Drug Issues, 2*, 133-151.

Pasupathi, M. (1999). Age differences in response to conformity pressure for emotional and nonemotional material. *Psychology and Aging, 14*, 170-174.

*Povey, R., Conner, M., Sparks, P., James, R., & Shepherd, R. (2000). The theory of planned behaviour and healthy eating: Examining additive and moderating effects of social influence variables. *Psychology and Health, 14*, 991-1006.

*Rivis, A., & Sheeran, P. (2001a). Integrating the theory of planned behaviour and the prototype/willingness model: Evidence for a direct relationship between prototypes and behaviour (manuscript under review).

*Rivis, A., & Sheeran, P. (2001b). Predicting young people's intentions to exercise: The importance of prototype similarity (manuscript under review).

Rosenthal, R. R., (1984). *Meta-analytic Procedures for Social Research.* Beverley Hills, CA: Sage.

*Schaalma, H., Kok, G., & Peters, L. (1993). Determinants of consistent condom use by adolescents: The impact of experience of sexual intercourse. *Health Education Research, 8*, 255-269.

Schwarzer, R. (1988). *Meta: Programs for Secondary Data Analysis.* Berlin: Free University of Berlin.

Sebald, H. (1989). Adolescents' peer orientation: Changes in the support system during the past three decades. *Adolescence, 24*, 937-946.

Sheeran, P. (2002). Intention-behaviour relations: A conceptual and empirical review. In W. Stroebe and M. Hewstone (Eds.), *European Review of Social Psychology,* Vol. 12 (pp. 1-36). London: John Wiley & Sons.

*Sheeran, P., & Orbell, S. (1999). Augmenting the theory of planned behavior: Roles for anticipated regret and descriptive norms. *Journal of Applied Social Psychology, 23*, 2107-2142.

Sheeran P., & Orbell, S. (1998). Do intentions predict condom use? Meta-analysis and examination of six moderator variables. *British Journal of Social Psychology, 37*, 231-250.

Sheeran, P., & Taylor, S. (1997). Predicting intentions to use condoms: Meta-analysis and comparison of the theories of reasoned action and planned behavior. *Journal of Applied Social Psychology, 29*, 1624-1675.

Snyder, C. R., & Fromkin, H. L. (1980). *Uniqueness: The pursuit of difference.* New York: Plenum.

*Stanton, B. F., Li, X., Black, M. M., Ricardo, I., Galbraith, J., Feigelman, S., & Kaljee, L. (1996). Longitudinal stability and predictability of sexual perceptions, intentions, and behaviors among early adolescent African-Americans. *Journal of Adolescent Health, 18*, 10-19.

Suls, J., & Mullen, B. (1982). From the cradle to the grave: Comparison and self-evaluation across the life span. In J. Suls (Ed.), *Psychological perspectives on the self* (Vol. 1, pp. 97-125). Hillsdale, NJ: Erlbaum.

Sutton, S. (1998). Predicting and explaining intentions and behavior: How well are we doing? *Journal of Applied Social Psychology, 28*, 1317-1338.

*Terry, D. J., & Hogg, M. A. (1996). Group norms and the attitude-behavior relationship: A role for group identification. *Personality and Social Psychology Bulletin, 22*, 776-793.

Trafimow, D. (1994). Predicting intentions to use a condom from perceptions of normative pressure and confidence in those perceptions. *Journal of Applied Social Psychology, 24*, 2151-2163.

Trafimow, D., & Sheeran, P. (1998). Some tests of the distinction between cognitive and affective beliefs. *Journal of Experimental Social Psychology, 34*, 378-397.

*White, K. M., Terry, D. J., & Hogg, M. A. (1994). Safer sex behavior: The role of attitudes, norms and control factors. *Journal of Applied Social Psychology, 24*, 2164-2192.

5

Eliciting Salient Beliefs in Research on the Theory of Planned Behavior: The Effect of Question Wording

Stephen Sutton, David P. French, Susie J. Hennings, Jo Mitchell, Nicholas J. Wareham, Simon Griffin, Wendy Hardeman, Ann Louise Kinmonth

The theory of reasoned action (TRA; Ajzen & Fishbein, 1980; Fishbein & Ajzen, 1975) and its extension, the theory of planned behavior (TPB; Ajzen, 1991; Ajzen & Madden, 1986) have been used to predict and explain a wide range of behaviors in terms of a limited set of constructs (attitude toward the behavior, subjective norm, perceived behavioral control, and behavioral intention). In these theories, salient beliefs are accorded an important role. Salient behavioral beliefs (beliefs about the consequences of performing the behavior) are held to determine attitude toward the behavior. Salient normative beliefs (beliefs about the views of significant others) are held to determine subjective norm. And salient control beliefs (beliefs about factors that may facilitate or impede performance of the behavior) are assumed to determine perceived behavioral control. *Salient* beliefs are those that first come to mind when respondents are asked open-ended questions such as "What do you think would be the advantages for you of performing behavior X?" They are also referred to as *accessible* beliefs (Ajzen & Fishbein, 2000; Higgins, 1996).

The TRA and the TPB are specified at the level of the individual. For example, the theories hold that individuals' salient behavioral beliefs determine their attitude toward the behavior. In practice, however, it is more convenient to identify the set of beliefs that are salient in a given population (Ajzen & Fishbein, 1980, p. 68). These *modal salient beliefs* can be identified by conducting an *elicitation study* in a representative sample of the population. The responses to a series of open-ended questions are recorded and a content analysis is conducted. Those beliefs that are elicited most frequently are included in the modal set and are used as the basis for the quantitative measures of beliefs.

In spite of the importance of salient beliefs in the TRA/TPB, the elicitation stage has received relatively little attention from researchers. The present paper examines whether altering the wording of the open-ended questions used to elicit modal behavioral beliefs results in different kinds of outcomes being mentioned. In particular, we compare the beliefs elicited by open-ended questions that have an *instrumental* and an *affective* focus respectively. A distinction between instrumental and affective components of attitude has been made in a number of papers on the TRA/TPB (e.g., Ajzen & Driver, 1991, 1992; Ajzen & Timko, 1986; Godin, 1987; Manstead & Parker, 1985; Valois, Desharnais, & Godin, 1988), but only two of these studies employed different questions to try to elicit different kinds of behavioral beliefs (Ajzen & Driver, 1991, 1992; Manstead & Parker, 1995). These will be discussed in turn.

Prior to their main study, which examined beliefs as predictors of participation in various recreational activities such as biking and mountain climbing, Ajzen and Driver (1991) conducted an elicitation study in which they identified salient instrumental and affective beliefs with respect to each activity. In order to elicit instrumental beliefs, participants were asked "What are the possible *costs* or *losses* of [mountain climbing]?" and "What are the possible *benefits* or *gains* of [mountain climbing]?" To elicit affective beliefs, respondents were asked to list the things they liked or enjoyed about each activity, and the things they disliked or hated about the activity. Ajzen and Driver (1991) listed the modal salient behavioral beliefs for two activities, mountain climbing and boating; these are given in table 5.1.

They note that there is some overlap between affective and instrumental beliefs for mountain climbing. In particular, a sense of accomplishment and feeling tired and exhausted appeared in both sets of beliefs. Behavioral beliefs with respect to boating, on the

Table 5.1
Salient Behavioral Beliefs Identified by Ajzen and Driver (1991) for Two Recreational Activities

Activity	Salient behavioral beliefs
Mountain climbing	Instrumental beliefs
	Improved physical fitness
	Developing experience and skills
	Endangering your life
	Experience nature and the outdoors
	A sense of accomplishment
	Physical injury (pulled muscles, broken bones)
	Being tired and exhausted
	Affective beliefs
	Being scared of height and danger
	Experiencing the views and scenery
	Feeling tired and exhausted
	Experiencing a sense of accomplishment
	Getting a serious workout
Boating (Sailing, canoeing, etc.)	Instrumental beliefs
	Endangering your life (drowning)
	Improved physical fitness
	Problems with equipment (motor, sails)
	Being relaxed
	Losing your way
	A sense of accomplishment
	Affective beliefs
	Feeling a cool breeze and spray of water
	A feeling of motion and freedom
	Being afraid of capsizing
	A feeling of solitude

other hand, showed no overlap. Ajzen and Driver (1991) also found evidence that instrumental and affective beliefs were differentially predictive of behavior assessed by self-report about one year later. For boating, for example, all four affective beliefs correlated significantly with frequency of boating, but only one of the six instrumental beliefs ("Endangering your life [drowning]") did so. In a review of their research applying the TPB to driving violations such as speeding in a built-up area, Manstead and Parker (1995) point out that the open-ended questions that are recommended by Ajzen and Fishbein (1980) to identify modal salient behavioral beliefs (which refer to "advantages" and "disadvantages") are likely to elicit instrumental beliefs (e.g., "Driving very fast increases the likelihood of having an accident") rather than affective beliefs (e.g., "Driving very fast is exciting"), thus yielding a biased set of modal salient beliefs. They briefly describe a pilot study in which they attempted to elicit both kinds of beliefs with respect to committing various driving violations, using questions similar to those employed by Ajzen and Driver (1991). Manstead and Parker give few details but they report that responses to the two sets of questions did not overlap at all: "When asked what they liked or disliked about speeding, respondents variously indicated that speeding made them feel exhilarated, or nervous, or powerful, or frightened, and so on. When asked the "standard" questions about the advantages and disadvantages of speeding, respondents indicated that speeding reduces journey times, can cause an accident, might result in being stopped by the police, and so on." (p. 90).

The present paper builds on the work of Ajzen and Driver (1991) and Manstead and Parker (1995) by reporting a detailed analysis of beliefs about "being more physically active in the next 12 months." The beliefs were elicited in a pilot study designed to guide the development of a quantitative TPB questionnaire for use in a randomised controlled trial of an intervention to increase physical activity among people at increased risk of diabetes (the ProActive trial). Physical activity is a domain in which affective outcomes (e.g., the pleasure of breathing fresh air or the discomfort of being hot and sweaty) might be expected to be as, or more, important influences on behavior than instrumental outcomes such as weight reduction or reduction in cardiovascular risk. Indeed, several of the papers cited above that examined the distinction between affective and instrumental components of attitude investigated physical exercise (e.g., Valois et al., 1988). In particular, we compare the beliefs that were elicited by questions designed to prompt instrumental outcomes (advantages and disadvantages) and affective outcomes (like or enjoy, dislike or hate). We also explore whether differences in elicited beliefs result in different final sets of modal salient beliefs. This will depend partly on the rule used for deciding which beliefs to include. Ajzen and Fishbein (1980) suggest three rules:

1. Include the ten or twelve most frequently mentioned outcomes. According to Ajzen and Fishbein (1980), this procedure results in a set of beliefs that is likely to include at least some of the beliefs mentioned by each respondent in the sample.
2. Include those beliefs that exceed a particular frequency, for example all beliefs mentioned by at least 10 percent or 20 percent of the sample.
3. Choose as many beliefs as necessary to account for a certain percentage (e.g., 75 percent) of all beliefs elicited. Ajzen and Fishbein suggest that this is the "least arbitrary rule," though they do not say why.

Finally, we examine the beliefs elicited by questions designed to prompt salient barriers and facilitators (control beliefs), and compare these with the instrumental and affective beliefs. For completeness, we also report the salient normative referents.

Method

Participants

The sample comprised 243 individuals drawn from two population-based sampling frames in Ely, Cambridgeshire, who attended the Ely Research Centre between December 1999 and October 2000 for a series of tests to measure energy expenditure, fitness, and glucose tolerance (Wareham, Hennings, Prentice & Day, 1997; Wareham, Wong & Day, 2000). Two hundred and thirteen (87.7 percent) people completed the questionnaire relevant to the present study. Twelve people were unable or unwilling to complete the tests (including the questionnaire), three people completed the tests but refused to complete the questionnaire, and fifteen people were excluded from the exercise component because of health reasons. Participants ranged in age from thirty-five to seventy-five years (mean 51.5, sd 10.4). The breakdown by socio-economic group was: professional 6.1 percent; managers and executives 22.5 percent; other non-manual 26.8 percent; skilled manual 21.6 percent; semi-skilled manual 9.9 percent; unskilled manual 8.9 percent; armed forces 1.4 percent; missing 2.8 percent. There were ninety-five men and 115 women (44.6 percent and 54.0 percent respectively; 1.4 percent missing). Participants and non-participants did not differ significantly on these variables.

Procedure

The open-ended questions were included at the beginning of a self-completion questionnaire entitled "Attitudes to Physical Activity." This was given to participants by a research nurse to complete in her presence at the end of the testing session. The introductory paragraph explained that "'more physically active' means doing anything that makes you more active, for example: walking faster or further than you do now; walking or cycling instead of taking the car; climbing the stairs more often; doing more gardening or D-I-Y."

The questions used are shown in table 5.2. Questions 1, 2, 5, and 6 were based on those recommended by Ajzen and Fishbein (1980), and the remainder on questions used by Ajzen and Driver (1991). Each question was followed by five lines numbered 1 to 5 for participants, to write in their responses. The order of the instrumental and affective questions was balanced. For approximately half the participants the questions appeared in the order shown in table 5.2;

Table 5.2 Open-Ended Questions Used in the Present Study.

---

1. What do you think would be the *advantages* for you of being more physically active in the next 12 months?
2. What do you think would be the *disadvantages* for you of being more physically active in the next 12 months?
3. What would you *like or enjoy* about being more physically active in the next 12 months?
4. What would you *dislike or hate* about being more physically active in the next 12 months?
5. Are there any groups or people who would *approve* of you being more physically active in the next 12 months?
6. Are there any groups or people who would *disapprove* of you being more physically active in the next 12 months?
7. What do you think would make it *difficult* for you to be more physically active in the next 12 months?
8. What do you think would make it *easy* for you to be more physically active in the next 12 months?

for the other half, questions 3 and 4 were moved to the beginning. The first twenty-seven questionnaires were used to develop the coding frame for each question. It was decided to use the same frame for the "like or enjoy" and "advantages" questions. Similarly, identical coding frames were used for the "dislike or hate" and "disadvantages" questions and for the "approve" and "disapprove" questions. On the other hand, somewhat different frames were required for the "easy" and "difficult" questions. Using these frames, the remaining 186 questionnaires were independently coded by two researchers. The values of Cohen's kappa ranged from 0.65 to 0.92 (table 5.3). The main source of disagreement was that coder A used the "Other, unclassifiable, miscellaneous" category more often than coder B. Given the acceptable level of agreement, it was decided to base the analysis on A's codes.

Results

Number of Responses

As table 5.3 shows, the total number of responses ranged from 48 to the "disapprove" question to 449 to the "advantages" question, that is from 0.23 to 2.11 responses per person. Very few people listed five or more responses, suggesting that participants were not constrained by the response format.

Table 5.3
Descriptive Statistics for Beliefs Elicited by the Eight Open-Ended Questions

Question	Total beliefs	Mean (SD) beliefs per person	No. (%) of people who gave 5 or more beliefs	Cohen's kappa
Like or enjoy	397	1.86 (1.51)	1.86 (1.51)	0.68
Advantages	449	2.11 (1.40)	2.11 (1.40)	0.72
Dislike or hate	141	0.66 (0.87)	0.66 (0.87)	0.75
Disadvantages	159	0.75 (1.02)	0.75 (1.02)	0.73
Approve	214	1.00 (1.05)	1.00 (1.05)	0.92
Disapprove	48	0.23 (.62)	0.23 (.62)	0.91
Easy	242	1.14 (0.88)	1.14 (0.88)	0.65
Difficult	277	1.30 (0.97)	1.30 (0.97)	0.83

There was a significant order effect. When the affective questions were placed at the beginning of the questionnaire, before the instrumental questions, significantly more beliefs were elicited in response to the "like or enjoy" question than when the order was reversed: means 2.23 (1.66) and 1.48 (1.23), $t(211) = 3.8$, $p < .001$. There were no significant order effects on the number of beliefs elicited in response to the other open-ended questions. Furthermore, there was little evidence that the actual content of the elicited beliefs was influenced by order of presentation. This factor is therefore ignored in the remaining analyses.

"Like or Enjoy" and "Advantages"

Table 5.4 shows the coding frame for the "like or enjoy" and "advantages" questions, and, for each category in turn, the number and percentage of participants who gave a response that fell into that category.[1]

Inspection of table 5.4 shows that, for both "like or enjoy" and "advantages," a substantial minority of participants (18.3 percent and 14.1 percent respectively) did not list any salient outcomes (Categories Y and Z), and a further 22.5 percent and 23.9 percent respectively gave responses that could not be classified (Category X). There were no significant differences between the "like or enjoy" and "advantages" questions on categories X, Y, or Z[2]. Other categories, however, did show significant differences. The "like or enjoy" question elicited responses in category A ("Would do intrinsically enjoyable activities") from one quarter of participants. Examples included: "being out in the fresh air," "walking more with the dog," "it's fun," and "would enjoy being able to swim more." Substantially fewer participants (7.0 percent) gave similar responses to the "advantages" question.

On the other hand, significantly more participants gave responses to the "advantages" question in categories B, C, E, and I. Responses classified in category B ("Better appearance") included "slimmer," "look better," and "appearance," but the majority referred to weight loss or weight control. category C ("General increase fitness/stamina/ capacity") included "not feel so tired," "having more energy," and "better stamina," but most responses used the words "fit," "fitter," or "fitness." Similarly, most of the responses coded in category E ("Improve health [not otherwise specified]") used the words "health,"

Table 5.4
Coding Frame for the "Like or Enjoy" and "Advantages" Questions, and
Numbers (Percentages) of Participants Who Gave Responses in Each Category

Category	Like or enjoy		Advantages	
A. Would do intrinsically enjoyable activities	52	(24.4%)	15	(7.0%)**
B. Better appearance	55	(25.8%)	85	(39.9%)**
C. General increase fitness/stamina/capacity	65	(30.5%)	95	(44.6%)**
D. Improved ability for specific intrinsic activities (e.g. work)	6	(2.8%)	8	(3.8%)
E. Improved health	22	(10.3%)	47	(22.1%)**
F. *Feeling* better	38	(17.8%)	38	(17.8%)
G. More mentally alert	4	(1.9%)	9	(4.2%)
H. Social and family aspects	18	(8.5%)	11	(5.2%)
I. Better sleeping/appetitie/less specific physical symptoms	9	(4.2%)	31	(14.6%)**
J. Feeling of achievement	2	(0.9%)	2	(0.9%)
X. Other, unclassifiable, miscellaneous	48	(22.5%)	51	(23.9%)
Y. None, nothing, can't think of anything, already doing enough excercise	35	(16.4%)	29	(13.6%)
Z. Missing	4	(1.9%)	1	(0.5%)

significance of difference in proportions: * $p < .05$ ** $p < .01$

"healthy" or "healthier," for example "feeling healthier," "better for my long term health," "health maintenance," and "general health improvement." Responses coded in category I ("Better sleeping/appetite/less specific physical symptoms") included "help me sleep," "lowering cholesterol levels," "improve osteoporosis," and "better resistance to colds etc."

"Dislike or Hate" and "Disadvantages"

Table 5.5 shows the coding frame that was used for the "dislike or hate" and "disadvantages" questions. A striking difference compared with table 5.4 is the large proportion of participants (52.5 percent for "dislike or hate" and 50.7 percent for "disadvantages") who did

Table 5.5
Coding Frame for the "Dislike or Hate" and "Disadvantages" Questions, and
Numbers (Percentages) of Participants Who Gave Responses in Each Category

Category	Dislike or Hate		Disadvantages	
A. Time Consuming	38	(17.8%)	15	(7.0%)
B. Difficult to fit in routine	2	(0.9%)	85	(39.9%)
C. Don't like it/don't like feeling hot, sweaty etc/cold, wet etc	22	(10.3%)	95	(44.6%)
D. Tiring/less rest	10	(4.7%)	8	(3.8%)
E. Motivation/effort	7	(3.3%)	47	(22.1%)
F. Boring/chore	9	(4.2%)	38	(17.8%)
G. Impaired work performance	0	(0.0%)	9	(4.2%)
H. Physical inability/strain or injuries	12	(5.6%)	11	(5.2%)
I. Staying overweight/gaining more weight	1	(0.5%)	31	(14.6%)
J. Money/material resources	3	(1.4%)	2	(0.9%)
X. Other, unclassifiable, miscellaneous	32	(15.0%)	51	(23.9%)
Y. None, nothing, can't think of anything, already doing enough excercise	100	(46.9%)	29	(13.6%)
Z. Missing	12	(5.6%)	1	(0.5%)

significance of difference in proportions: * $p < .05$ ** $p < .01$

not list any salient outcomes in response to the questions (Categories Y and Z). Taken together with the findings reported in the preceding section, this suggests that the sample had generally positive salient beliefs (and therefore generally positive attitudes) with respect to increasing physical activity. There were no significant differences between the "dislike or hate" and "disadvantages" questions on categories X or Y. However, there was a significant difference on category Z.

For both questions, the modal category was A ("Time consuming"). For "dislike or hate," 17.8 percent gave responses that were classified in this category; the corresponding figure for "disadvantages" was 21.6 percent. The wording used by respondents was very consistent: the word "time" was used in all but four cases. Typical responses were "finding time," "lack of time," and "losing the time."

There was no significant difference between the two questions on this category. However, the two questions did differ significantly on categories C, F, and H. Significantly more participants gave responses to the "dislike or hate" question in category C ("Don't like it/don't like feeling hot, sweaty etc./cold, wet etc."). Typical responses were "going out on cold evenings," "exerting myself," "getting hot and red," and "jogging." There was a difference in the same direction for category F (Boring/chore). Example responses were "being bored" and "If I felt that it had become a chore." By contrast, more participants gave responses in category H (Physical inability/strain or injuries) to the "disadvantages" question. Typical responses in this category were "my back," "stiff limbs and joints," and "may suffer angina pain."

Given the differences obtained between responses to the affective ("like or enjoy," "dislike or hate") and instrumental ("advantages," "disadvantages") questions, we examined whether this would materially affect the final set of modal salient beliefs. Table 5.6 shows the modal categories for the "advantages/disadvantages" and "like or enjoy/dislike or hate" questions according to two of the selection rules suggested by Ajzen and Fishbein (1980). The 20 percent rule yields four modal categories for the instrumental questions and three for the affective questions, but only two categories are common to both. In a study designed to investigate the relationship between behavioral beliefs and attitude toward the behavior, it is conceivable that different results would be obtained depending on which set of beliefs was used. Using the 10 percent rule gives seven modal categories for the instrumental questions and six for the affective questions, with five in common.

The 75 percent rule (choose as many beliefs as necessary to account for 75 percent of all beliefs elicited) yielded eleven modal categories for the affective questions and ten modal categories for the instrumental questions; there were ten categories in common. The "Top 10" rule (include the ten most frequently mentioned outcomes) yielded nine categories in common, and the "Top 12" rule yielded ten in common. Decision rules that lead to a larger number of categories being included would be expected to yield more similar sets of modal categories. In the extreme case, including the twenty most frequent categories would yield identical sets of modal categories (because there are twenty categories in total listed in tables 5.4 and 5.5).

Table 5.6
Modal Categories for Instrumental and Affective Questions that
Would be Selected Using Two Different Decision Rules

Rule	Advantages/Disadvantages	Like or enjoy/Dislike or hate
20% rule[a]	General increase fitness/stamina/ capacity Better appearance Improve health (not otherwise specified) Time consuming	General increase fitness/stamina/ capacity Better appearance Would do intrinsically enjoyable activities
10% rule[b]	General increase fitness/stamina/ capacity Better appearance Improve health (not otherwise specified) Time consuming *Feeling* better Better sleeping/appetite/less specific physical symptoms Physical inability/strain or injuries	General increase fitness/stamina/ capacity Better appearance Would do intrinsically enjoyable activities Time consuming *Feeling* better Improve health (not otherwise specified)

[a] Include a category only if at least 20% of participants gave responses that were coded in that category. [b] Include a category only if at least 10% of participants gave responses that were coded in that category.

"Approve" and "Disapprove"

In comparison with the other questions, responses to these questions were easy to categorise, with only a small proportion being coded in the miscellaneous category (table 5.7). A substantial minority of participants (38.5 percent) did not list any salient referents in response to the "approve" question. The modal responses to this question were "Husband/wife/partner," "Family (unspecified)," and "Children." A large majority of participants (85.5 percent) did not list any salient referents in response to the "disapprove" question. On the assumption that respondents are likely to list referents with whom they are motivated to comply, the findings for the "approve" and "disapprove" questions suggest that, on average, participants had positive subjective norms with respect to increasing physical activity.

Table 5.7
Coding Frame for the "Approve" and Disapprove" Questions, and Numbers
(Percentages) of Participants Who Gave Responses in Each Category

Category	Approve		Disapprove	
A. Husband/wife/partner	65	(30.5%)	12	(5.6%)**
B. Children	37	(17.4%)	9	(4.2%)**
C. Family (unspecified)	43	(20.2%)	5	(2.3%)**
D. Parents	6	(2.8%)	4	(1.9%)
E. Work colleagues	16	(7.5%)	5	(2.3%)*
F. Doctor/other health professional	17	(8.0%)	1	(0.5%)**
G. Friends	10	(4.7%)	1	(0.5%)*
X. Other, unclassifiable, miscellaneous	11	(5.2%)	5	(2.3%)
Y. None, nothing, can't think of anything, already doing enough exercise	78	(36.6%)	171	(80.3%)**
Z. Missing	4	(1.9%)	11	(5.2%)*

Significance of Difference in Proportions: * P < .05   ** P < .01

"Difficult" and "Easy"

Somewhat different coding frames were developed for the "easy" and "difficult" questions (tables 5.8 and 5.9). The responses elicited by the "easy" question were not simply the obverse of those elicited by the "difficult" question. For instance, a significant minority of participants (12.7 percent) gave responses to the "difficult" question that were classified as reflecting (low) motivation (Category F in table 5.8); typical examples were "getting over laziness," "my attitude to it," and "lack will power." However, similar responses were not elicited by the "easy" question. Nevertheless, there was some correspondence between the responses to the two questions, in particular in relation to time (category A in both tables 5.8 and 5.9), work (category D in table 5.8; category B in table 5.9), and health (category E in both tables). In spite of their position in the questionnaire—they were the last set of open-ended questions to be asked—the percentages of participants who did not list any salient barriers or facilitating factors were comparatively low (16.5 percent for "difficult" and 19.2 percent for "easy").

Combining categories for the two questions where appropriate, the modal responses were time (mentioned by 48.8 percent of participants), work (34.7 percent), and health (26.8 percent), followed by "Motivation" (12.7 percent; category F in table 4.8) and "Children/family commitments" (10.8 percent; category C in table 5.8).

Discussion

To our knowledge, this is the first paper on the TRA/TPB to report a detailed analysis of findings from the elicitation stage. In view of the important role accorded to salient beliefs by these theories – as the factors that causally influence attitude, subjective norm, perceived behavioral control and hence intention and behavior—it is surpris-

Table 5.8
Coding Frame for the "Difficult" Question, and Number (Percentage) of Participants Who Gave Responses in Each Category

Category		
A. Time	85	(39.9%)
B. Expense	4	(1.9%)
C. Children/family commitments	23	(10.8%)
D. Work commitments	43	(20.2%)
E. Physical/health limitations	42	(19.7%)
F. Motivation	27	(12.7%)
G. Tiredness	6	(2.8%)
X. Other, unclassifiable, miscellaneous	34	(16.0%)
Y. None, nothing, can't think of anything, already doing enough exercise	31	(14.6%)
Z. Missing	4	(1.9%)

Table 5.9
Coding Frame for the "Easy" Question, and Number (Percentage)
of Participants Who Gave Responses in Each Category

Category		
A. More time (not otherwise specified)	42	(19.7%)
B. Change/re-organisation/retirement from work	52	(24.4%)
C. Partner/family more supportive (e.g. with housework)	7	(3.3%)
D. Other people to exercise with	12	(5.6%)
E. Improvement in health/less tired	15	(7.0%)
F. Access to facilities easier/less barriers (e.g. better weather)	19	(8.9%)
G. Prioritize exercise/re-organise life	15	(7.0%)
H. More money/material resources	7	(3.3%)
X. Other, unclassifiable, miscellaneous	51	(23.9%)
Y. None, nothing, can't think of anything, already doing enough exercise	29	(13.6%)
Z. Missing	12	(5.6%)

ing that so little attention has been paid to the elicitation stage. We examined whether using different wordings for the open-ended questions resulted in different kinds of beliefs being elicited. Our findings showed that the beliefs that were elicited by questions designed to prompt affective outcomes (like or enjoy, dislike or hate) differed systematically from those that were elicited by the traditional questions designed to prompt instrumental outcomes (advantages and disadvantages). In particular, the "like or enjoy" question elicited references to doing intrinsically enjoyable activities (e.g., "would enjoy being able to swim more") from significantly more participants than the "advantages" question. On the other hand, the latter question elicited significantly more responses that were classified under better appearance, improved health, and increased fitness. These findings confirm those of Ajzen and Driver (1991) who investigated recreational activities such as boating and Manstead and Parker (1995) who studied driving violations, and extend them to a different behavioral domain.

We also examined the beliefs elicited by questions designed to prompt salient barriers and facilitating factors (control beliefs). These asked participants what they thought would make it "difficult" and what they thought would make it "easy" for them to be more physically active in the next twelve months. It is noteworthy that significant percentages of participants (39.9 percent and 19.7 percent respectively) mentioned time in response to these questions. Indeed, this was the modal response to the "difficult" question as it was to the "dislike or hate" and "disadvantages" questions. From a practical viewpoint, these findings suggest that beliefs about the time-consuming nature of physical activity are important, that they need to be adequately represented in quantitative questionnaires on this topic, and that interventions that aim to increase physical activity should address these beliefs.

We also investigated whether the differences in the beliefs elicited in response to the affective and instrumental questions resulted in different final sets of modal salient beliefs. This was found to depend on the particular decision rule that was employed. The 20 percent rule (include beliefs mentioned by at least 20 percent of participants) resulted in modal sets that overlapped but differed sufficiently to suggest that they might yield different findings in a quantitative study. As would be expected, more lenient decision rules yielded modal sets that were more similar to each other.

In the literature on the TRA/TPB, there has been little theoretical discussion or empirical comparison of the various decision rules. Our findings show that the different rules can yield very different sets of modal beliefs. How should an investigator decide which rule to use in a particular case? One possible criterion is the percentage of participants in the elicitation study who mention at least one belief in the modal set, which we will refer to as *coverage (people)*. Another is the percentage of the total beliefs elicited that fall in the modal set, which we will call *coverage (beliefs)*. (The latter criterion is also equal to the mean number of elicited beliefs per person that fall in the modal set divided by the mean total number of elicited beliefs per person.) Decision rules that yield a relatively large modal set will tend to be associated with greater coverage—of both people and beliefs—than rules that yield a relatively small modal set. For example, in the present dataset the 20 percent rule applied to responses to the "advantages" and "disadvantages" questions yielded four modal categories that covered 74.2 percent of participants and

48.8 percent of beliefs. The mean total number of beliefs elicited per person in response to the "advantages" and "disadvantages" questions was 2.85 (table 5.3). The mean number of these beliefs that fell in the modal set was 1.39. In comparison, the "Top 10" rule gave corresponding coverage figures of 78.9 percent and 75.3 percent, and the mean number of elicited beliefs per person that fell in the modal set was 2.15.

However, the greater coverage achieved by the more lenient "Top 10" rule incurs a cost. Suppose that a set of quantitative belief items based on the modal set were presented to a new sample of people assumed to hold the same salient beliefs as our elicitation sample. An estimate of each participant's indirect (i.e., belief-based) attitude could be derived in the usual way by computing the product of the belief strength and outcome evaluation for each belief in the modal set and summing these products across beliefs.[3] Each participant in the new sample could be thought of as having a "true" indirect attitude based on beliefs that are salient to them. Ideally, the estimated indirect attitude should correlate perfectly with the true indirect attitude across individuals, and the correlations between the estimated indirect attitude and measures of other components of the TRA/TPB (e.g., direct attitude) would then be equal to the corresponding correlations involving the true indirect attitude. The correlation between the estimated and true indirect attitude cannot be known, of course. However, the greater the overlap between the participants' salient beliefs and those in the modal set, the higher this correlation should be.

The degree of overlap will vary depending on the modal set. If the modal set were chosen using the 20 percent rule, each person in the new sample would be presented with four belief statements. On average, 1.39 of each individual's salient beliefs would fall in the modal set, but the other 1.46 (= 2.85 − 1.39; see above) would fall outside the modal set and so would be missed. Furthermore, the individual would be presented, on average, with 2.61 (= 4 − 1.39) belief statements that were not salient to him or her. If the modal set were chosen using the "Top 10" rule, each person in the new sample would be presented with, by definition, ten belief statements. On average, 2.15 of each individual's salient beliefs would fall in the modal set, and the other 0.70 (= 2.85 − 2.15) would fall outside the modal set and would thus be missed. However, each individual would now be presented, on average, with 7.85 (= 10 − 2.15) belief statements that were not personally salient.

Table 5.10
Indices for Different Sets of Modal Beliefs Relating to
"Advantages and Disadvantages"

Modal set	Hits[a]	Misses[b]	Non-salient beliefs[c]	Errors[d]	Hits/(Hits + Errors)
Top 1	0.53	2.33	0.47	2.80	0.16
Top 2	0.94	1.92	1.06	2.98	0.24
Top 3	1.17	1.69	1.83	3.52	0.25
Top 4	1.39	1.46	2.61	4.07	0.26
Top 5	1.58	1.28	3.42	4.70	0.25
Top 6	1.74	1.12	4.26	5.38	0.24
Top 7	1.90	0.96	5.10	6.06	0.24
Top 8	2.02	0.83	5.98	6.81	0.23
Top 9	2.09	0.76	6.91	7.68	0.21
Top 10	2.15	0.70	7.85	8.55	0.20
Top 11	2.19	0.66	8.81	9.47	0.19
Top 12	.23	0.62	9.77	10.39	0.18

[a] Mean number of salient beliefs per person that fall within the modal set.
[b] Mean number of salient beliefs per person that fall outside the modal set.
[c] Mean number of non-salient beliefs per person in the modal set.
[d] Sum of the preceding two columns.

It can be seen from the example outlined above that the choice of decision rules, leading to different numbers of modal beliefs, involves a trade-off between maximising the number of the person's salient beliefs that fall in the modal set (the number of "hits") and minimising the number of "errors" (omitting beliefs from the modal set that are salient to the individual, and including beliefs in the modal set that are not salient to him or her). The above analysis suggests a new decision rule: include in the modal set the number of beliefs that maximises the ratio of hits to hits plus errors. This ratio has a theoretical range of 0 to 1. A ratio of 0 indicates no overlap between the individual's salient beliefs and the beliefs in the modal set, and a ratio of 1 indicates complete overlap between these two sets. The last column of table 5.10 shows the value of this ratio for different modal sets of beliefs relating to "advantages and disadvantages" in the current dataset.[4] It can be seen that the "Top 4" set has the largest ratio (0.26). However, the "Top 2" set would be the preferred choice because it has a ratio that is only slightly lower (0.24) than the "Top 4" and it includes two fewer beliefs.

This method treats the two kinds of error as equally serious: failing to include a person's salient belief in the modal set is given equal weight to supplying him or her with a belief that is not salient. It can be argued that the second kind of error is potentially more serious than the first. When an individual who is completing a questionnaire is presented with a statement that refers to a belief that is not personally salient, it may become salient, and, since the TRA/TPB holds that attitude toward the behavior is determined by salient beliefs, this may lead to a change in attitude. In other words, presenting items that refer to non-salient beliefs may be reactive. The decision rule we have proposed can easily be adapted to give greater weight to one kind of error if required.

In this example, the optimal modal set ("Top 4") had only a 26 percent overlap with individuals' salient beliefs. It seems unlikely that this would be sufficient to yield an accurate estimate of indirect attitude in a similar sample in which participants were presented with quantitative belief items based on the modal set. Instead of supplying a standard set of modal salient beliefs derived from an elicitation study, an alternative approach is ask participants to generate their own beliefs about the target behavior and then to rate them in terms of belief strength and outcome evaluation. A measure of indirect attitude based on individually generated beliefs should provide a more accurate estimate of true indirect attitude (in the sense of having a higher correlation with true indirect attitude) than a measure based on a set of modal salient beliefs that has a relatively small degree of overlap with individuals' salient beliefs.

To our knowledge, only two studies have compared measures based on individually-generated and modal salient beliefs in terms of their correlations with measures of other components of the TRA/TPB (Agnew, 1998; Rutter & Bunce, 1989). The findings did not provide consistent support for the hypothesis that measures based on individually generated beliefs would yield higher correlations. Rutter and Bunce (1989) found that, compared with a measure of indirect attitude based on modal salient beliefs, a measure of indirect attitude based on individually generated beliefs correlated more highly with a measure of intention but not with a direct measure of attitude. (One criticism that can be levelled at this study is that, in computing the measure of indirect attitude based on the participant's own beliefs, the total score was divided by the number of beliefs; in fact, the sum, rather than the mean, should have been used, and might have yielded a different pattern of correlations.) Agnew (1998, p. 284) concluded from his findings that "Overall, subjects' ratings of their own behavioral and normative beliefs tended to provide marginally higher correlations with global measures of attitude toward behavior and subjective norm, although the relative magnitude of the differences among the correlations in most cases was modest."

More studies of this kind are needed in which behaviors and populations with different distributions of salient beliefs are investigated and the effect of different modal sets is examined. Among the issues that should be addressed in future research are the possible reactive effects of asking people to generate their own beliefs and the problem of deciding how many beliefs are salient for a given individual.

Conclusions

Using different wordings for the open-ended questions in an elicitation study may result in different kinds of beliefs being elicited. Whether this makes any material difference to the final set of modal salient beliefs may depend on the particular decision rule that is employed. A number of such rules have been suggested by Ajzen and Fishbein (1980) but none of them has an explicit rationale. We proposed an alternative decision rule that is based on maximising the degree of overlap between the modal set and individuals' salient beliefs. The index of overlap can be used to gauge the adequacy of using a modal set of a given size to represent the salient beliefs of the whole sample. In the current dataset, the optimal modal set for "advantages and disadvantages" was associated with only 26 percent overlap, which was judged to be insufficient. In such cases, a better strategy may be to ask participants to generate and rate their own beliefs.

Notes

1.   Note that it would also have been possible to present the results in terms of the number of *responses* per category rather than the number of *participants* per category (because some participants gave two or more responses that were coded in the same category). However, the pattern of findings was broadly similar in the two cases, and treating the participant as the unit of analysis avoids problems arising from statistical dependency of observations.
2.   For comparing proportions in paired samples we used the test recommended by Newcombe and Altman (2000) and implemented in the program Confidence Inter-

val Analysis. In every case, the test gave similar results to the traditional (McNemar's) test.
3.   In this discussion we ignore the problems that arise from the use of multiplicative composites (see Evans, 1991, and French & Hankins, in press).
4.   These ratios are derived from the aggregated data. It would also be possible to compute ratios for each individual in the sample.

References

Agnew, C.R. (1998). Modal versus individually-derived beliefs about condom use: Measuring the cognitive underpinnings of the theory of reasoned action. *Psychology and Health, 13,* 271-287.

Ajzen, I. (1991). The theory of planned behavior. *Organizational Behavior and Human Decision Processes, 50,* 179-211.

Ajzen, I., & Driver, B. L. (1991). Prediction of leisure participation from behavioral, normative, and control beliefs: An application of the theory of planned behavior. *Leisure Sciences, 13,* 185-204.

Ajzen, I., & Driver, B. L. (1992). Application of the theory of planned behavior to leisure choice. *Journal of Leisure Research, 24,* 207-224.

Ajzen, I., Fishbein. M. (1980). *Understanding attitudes and predicting social behavior.* Englewood Cliffs, NJ: Prentice-Hall.

Ajzen, I., & Fishbein M. (2000). Attitudes and the attitude-behavior relation: Reasoned and automatic processes. *European Review of Social Psychology, 11,* 1-33.

Ajzen, I., & Madden, T. J. (1986). Prediction of goal-directed behaviour: Attitudes, intention, and perceived behavioural control. *Journal of Experimental Social Psychology, 22,* 453-474.

Ajzen, I., & Timko, C. (1986). Correspondence between health attitudes and behavior. *Basic and Applied Social Psychology, 7,* 259-276.

Evans, M. G. (1991). The problem of analyzing multiplicative composites. *American Psychologist, 46,* 6-15.

Fishbein, M., & Ajzen, I. (1975). *Belief, attitude, intention, and behavior: An introduction to theory and research.* Reading, MA: Addison-Wesley.

French, D. P., & Hankins, M. (in press). The expectancy-value muddle in the theory of planned behavior —and some proposed solutions. *British Journal of Health Psychology.*

Godin, G. (1987). Importance of the emotional aspect of attitude to predict intention. *Psychological Reports, 61,* 719-723.

Higgins, E. T. (1996). Knowledge activation: Accessibility, applicability, and salience. In E. T. Higgins, & A. W. Kruglanski (Eds.), *Social psychology: Handbook of basic principles.* pp. 133-168. New York: The Guilford Press.

Manstead, A. S. R., & Parker, D. (1995). Evaluating and extending the theory of planned behaviour. *European Review of Social Psychology, 6,* 69-95.

Newcombe, R. G., & Altman, D. G. (2000). Proportions and their differences. In D. G. Altman, D. Machin, T. N. Bryant, & M. J. Gardner (Eds.), *Statistics with confidence* (2nd ed.). pp. 45-56. London: BMJ books.

Rutter, D. R., & Bunce, D. J. (1989). The theory of reasoned action of Fishbein and Ajzen: A test of Towriss's amended procedure for measuring beliefs. *British Journal of Social Psychology, 28,* 39-46.

Valois, P., Desharnais, R., & Godin, G. (1988). A comparison of the Fishbein and Ajzen and the Triandis attitudinal models for the prediction of exercise intention and behavior. *Journal of Behavioral Medicine, 11,* 459-472.

Wareham. N. J., Hennings, S.J., Prentice, A. M., & Day, N. E. (1997). Feasibility of heart-rate monitoring to estimate total level and pattern of energy expenditure in a population-based epidemiological study: The Ely young cohort feasibility study 1994-5. *British Journal of Nutrition*, 78, 889-900.

Wareham, N. J., Wong, M.-Y., & Day, N. E. (2000). Glucose intolerance and physical inactivity: The relative importance of low habitual energy expenditure and cardiorespiratory fitness. *American Journal of Epidemiology*, 152, 132-139.

6

Examining Normative Pressure in the Theory of Planned Behavior: Impact of Gender and Passengers on Intentions to Break the Speed Limit

Mark Conner, Neil Smith, and Brian McMillan

Introduction

The present research was concerned with an application of the Theory of Planned Behavior (TPB; Ajzen, 1991) to a "risky" driving behavior (i.e., speeding) in a sample of young people. Such behaviors are reported to be common in this group and to be significantly more common in males compared to females (Baxter, Manstead, Stradling, Campbell, Reason, & Parker, 1990; Harre, Field, & Kirkwood, 1996). Such behaviors are also reported to vary as a function of the presence of passengers (Baxter et al., 1990). In addition, previous research (Parker, Manstead, Stradling, Reason, & Baxter, 1992b) has indicated that normative pressure is the strongest predictor of intentions to perform these behaviors. Hence, the present research examined the impact of passenger type (number and gender) on intentions to speed in young men and women. In addition, we took the opportunity to examine the moderating effects of gender and passenger type on relationships in the TPB for this behavior. Of particular interest was how gender and passenger type might moderate the impact of normative pressure on intentions to perform this behavior.

The present study focussed on the risky driving behavior of exceeding the posted speed limit (speeding). This behavior is related to increased accident risk (Parker et al., 1992b). The approach examined respondents' judgments about a written hypothetical driving scenario whilst imagining themselves alone, with a passenger of the same sex, with a passenger of the opposite sex, or with a group of passengers. Such hypothetical scenarios allow careful control over the information each respondent receives, and allow one to manipulate factors such as the presence of passengers in the scenario, and examine how respondent characteristics influence their responses (Hughes, 1998). This methodology has been successfully used by a number of other social psychologists to study driving (e.g., Parker et al., 1992b; Parker, Manstead, & Stradling, 1995) and other behaviors (e.g., Conner & Flesch, 2001; Conner, Graham, & Moore, 1999; Leigh, Aramburu, & Norris, 1992; Leigh & Aramburu, 1996). A focus on intentions rather than behavior is a necessary consequence of the selection of this methodology. However, intentions are moderately strongly positively correlated with behavior across a variety of domains (e.g., Sheppard, Hartwick, & Warshaw, 1988, report an average intention-behavior correlation of .53 across the 88 studies reviewed).

Theory of Planned Behavior

In the Theory of Planned Behavior (TPB: Ajzen, 1985, 1991; see Armitage & Conner, 2001 for a meta-analytic review) intentions represent a person's motivation or conscious plan or decision to exert effort to perform the behavior. Intentions are determined by three sets of variables. The first is attitudes, which are based on perceived likelihood and evaluation of salient outcomes. The second is subjective norms, which are based on the person's perceptions of whether specific salient others think he/she should engage in the behavior and the motivation to comply with such pressure (i.e., normative pressure). The third predictor is perceived behavioral control (PBC), which is based upon the individual's perception of the extent to which factor facilitate or inhibit performance of the behavior and their frequency of occurrence.

The TPB has been applied to the prediction of a number of different behaviors with some success (Ajzen, 1991; Conner & Sparks, 1996; Godin & Kok, 1996). These include driving behaviors in a number of studies (e.g. Parker et al., 1995; Parker, Manstead, Stradling, & Reason, 1992a; Parker et al., 1992b; Parker, Stradling, & Manstead, 1996). Parker et al. (1992b) used the TPB to help understand intentions to speed (the behavior used here) amongst other driving behaviors. Subjective norms were the strongest predictors of intentions for this behavior.

Whilst the TPB is held to be a complete model of the proximal determinants of behavior (i.e., all other influences are assumed to exert their impact upon behavior via changes in components of the model), a number of other predictors of intentions have also been reported in the literature (see Conner & Armitage, 1998). Three additional variables were examined in the present paper: past behavior, moral norms and anticipated affective reactions.

Additional Variables

The role of past behavior in the TPB has attracted considerable attention (see Eagly & Chaiken, 1993, pp. 178-182 for a review). The TPB predicts that the impact of past behavior on intentions is mediated by the TPB variables and PBC in particular (Ajzen, 1991). However, several studies have reported independent effects for past behavior in the TPB (Bagozzi & Kimmel, 1995; Conner, Warren, Close, & Sparks, 1999; Godin, Valois, & Lepage, 1993; Norman & Smith, 1995). Such findings support calls for past behavior to be considered as an independent predictor of intentions (Bentler & Speckart, 1979; Sutton, 1994). Moral obligations or norms are perceptions of the degree of moral correctness of a behavior (Ajzen, 1991; Manstead, 1999) and take account of , "....*personal* feelings of ..... responsibility to perform, or refuse to perform, a certain behavior" (Ajzen, 1991, p.199). Several studies have found moral norms to be predictive of intentions over and above the components of the TPB (e.g., Beck & Ajzen, 1991; Sparks, Shepherd, & Frewer, 1995) including driving behaviors (Parker et al., 1995).

Anticipated affective reactions can also be an important determinant of behavior. The concept of anticipated regret (Parker et al., 1995; Richard, van der Pligt, & de Vries, 1995, 1996a, 1996b) has been a focus of several studies. These studies indicate that indicate that individuals who anticipate feeling regret after performing a behavior are less likely to perform the behavior or intend to perform the behavior.

Research Aims

This research investigated the effect of the components of the TPB and three additional predictors (past behavior, moral norms, anticipated affective reactions) on intentions to speed. The study examined men and women's intentions and manipulated the presence of a passenger (and type of passenger). The analyses focus on differences in measured variables between men and women in these different conditions and the moderating influence of gender and passenger on the relationship between measured variables and intentions.

Method

Participants and Procedure

The participants were a convenience sample of Leeds University students and Leeds residents recruited individually around campus. Of the 200 distributed questionnaires, a total of 170 completed questionnaires were returned (85 percent response rate). Eight questionnaires were incomplete, leaving a useable sample of 162 respondents (eighty-three females; seventy-nine males; age $M=20.9$ years, $SD=1.69$). Each privately read one scenario on speeding and completed an anonymous questionnaire whilst imagining themselves in the given scenario, and returned these to the researcher. One of four scenarios (travelling alone, accompanied by a passenger of the same age and sex, accompanied by a passenger of the opposite sex but the same age, accompanied by a group of passengers of the same age) was randomly presented to respondents. The scenario describing the travelling alone and speeding condition is given below:

> You are driving alone a dual carriageway which you know has pedestrian crossings at various points along it. You are driving alone. It is a fine, dry day and the traffic in your opinion is moving too slowly. Therefore you decide to move into the outside lane and exceed the 40 mph speed limit by 20 mph.

Measures

A number of measures were used in the questionnaire. TPB components were measured by a number of multi-item scales in relation to driving in the manner described. For the belief-based measures, the beliefs were those modally salient beliefs by Parker et al. (1992b) in previous research with a sample of UK adults. Respondents initially recorded age and sex and then the following variables in relation to the scenario presented.

Intentions to drive in the manner described were assessed by four items (e.g., "How likely would it be for you to speed in this situation," highly unlikely—highly likely; *alpha*= 0.85). The items were scored between -3 and +3 (higher scored indicating a stronger intention to speed) and averaged.

Behavioral beliefs and evaluations of the outcomes of driving in the manner described were assessed by five items for speeding and six items for close following (e.g., "Speeding in this situation would get me to my destination quicker," very unlikely—very likely; "Getting to my destination quicker would be....," very bad—very good). The outcomes were: get to destination quicker, cause a pedestrian accident, break the law, cause an accident, and passing slower cars more quickly. All items were scored between -3 (very unlikely or bad) and +3 (extremely likely or good) and corresponding outcome beliefs and evaluations multiplicatively combined and then an average computed. Hence, scores range between -9 and +9 for each individual, with positive scores indicating overall positive outcomes and negative scores indicating overall negative outcomes.

Normative beliefs and motivations to comply were each assessed by seven items (7 x 2 items; e.g., "How would the police react to you driving in the manner described," strongly disapprove—strongly approve; "I generally like to drive in the way that the police would approve of," strongly disagree—strongly agree). The referent groups were police, other drivers, my passengers, the typical young male driver, my partner, my family, my close friends and an impatient driver. The normative belief items were scored -3 to +3 with higher scores indicating greater motivation to comply. Corresponding items were multiplicatively combined and an average for each subject computed; thus scores could range between -21 and +21, with higher scores indicating greater pressure to speed.

Control beliefs and power were assessed by nine items (e.g., "Would you be more likely or less likely to carry out this manoeuvre if it was night time," much less likely—much more likely; "How often do you encounter darkness when driving," never – frequently). The control factors were : darkness, wet roads, heavy traffic, passengers in your car, being in a bad mood, being in a rush, being in a good mood, icy conditions, misty weather. These items were each scored between-3 and +3 (higher scores indicating greater perceptions of factors facilitating speeding or being more frequent), multiplicatively combined and averaged.

Anticipated affective reaction of driving in the manner described were assessed by two pairs of items (e.g., "Speeding in this situation would cause me to feel regret," very unlikely—very likely; "Feeling regret at my action would be ....," very bad—very good). The outcomes were feel regret and feel exhilarated. Items were scored between -3 (very unlikely or bad) and +3 (extremely likely or good), multiplicatively combined and an average computed. Hence, scores range between -9 and +9 for each individual, with positive scores indicating overall positive feelings.

Moral norms was assessed by a single item (e.g., "It would be quite wrong for me to speed in this situation," strongly disagree - strongly agree). The item was scored between -3 and +3 (higher scores indicate greater moral norm not to speed).

Past behavior was assessed by asking how often the behavior was performed in different conditions (e.g., "How often do you speed when travelling alone," never—nearly always). The conditions were : driving alone, accompanied by a male of the same age, accompanied by a female of the same age, and accompanied by a group of people. The items were scored between 1 to 7 with higher scores indicating greater frequency and averaged (*alpha*=0.89).

Results

Table 6.1 presents descriptive data (*M* and *SD*) and intercorrelations for the study variables. In general, the measures were not excessively skewed and showed reasonable levels of variation. Examination of the intercorrelations indicated that past behavior and control beliefs were the best predictors of intentions to *speed.*

Table 6.2 shows the descriptive data (*M* and *SD*) for male and female respondents in each of the driving groups. A 2 (sex) by 4 (group) MANOVA was performed to test for significant differences. For *speeding,* there was a significant multivariate effect for sex (*Pillais F* (7, 144) = 2.62, $p < 0.01$), but no effects for group (*Pillais F*(21, 438) = 0.63) or the sex by group interaction (*Pillais F*(21, 438) = 1.12). Examination of the univariate effects for sex revealed effects for normative beliefs ($F(1, 150) = 2.83$, $p =0.09$), control beliefs ($F(1, 150) = 7.33$, $p < 0.01$), and moral norms ($F(1, 150) = 3.18$, $p = 0.07$). Examination of the means for normative beliefs indicated that while both males and females reported social pressure not to speed, this pressure was greater in women than men. For control beliefs, there were generally perceived to be more facilitating than inhibiting factors for speeding, but men reported more

Table 6.1
Descriptive Data and Correlations among Measures (N = 158)

	1.	2.	3.	4.	5.	6.	7.	M	(SD)
1. Intention	-	0.39	0.33	0.43	.26	-.35	.44	-0.20	(1.41)
2. Behavioural beliefs		-	.31	.29	.16	-.29	.13	-2.33	(1.85)
3. Normative beliefs			-	.31	.16	-.18	-.07	-3.84	(4.73)
4. Control beliefs				-	.25	-.18	.22	0.86	(3.23)
5. Anticipated affective reaction					-	-.19	.04	-0.58	(2.09)
6. Moral norms						-	-.18	0.62	(1.74)
7. Past Behavior							-	4.59	(1.28)

For correlations greater than 0.16, $p < 0.05$; for correlations greater than 0.21, $p < 0.01$; for correlations greater than
0.26, $p < 0.01$; for correlations greater than 0.26, $p < 0.001$, all two-tailed.

facilitators. Finally, respondents generally perceived a moral norm not to speed, however, in contrast to the previous findings women reported a greater moral norm not to speed than men.

In the next analysis, we regressed intentions onto the predictor variables. In addition to the overall regression, we also computed regressions for each sex by passenger combination. The results of these regressions are shown in table 6.3. *For speeding intentions,* the overall regression showed all variables except anticipated affective reaction to be significant. Stronger intentions to speed were associated with perceiving that this would lead to positive outcomes, that it would meet with social approval, that factors facilitated it's performance, that there was little moral obligation not to speed, and that one had speeded frequently in the past. This regression accounted for 45 percent of the variance in intentions.

Table 6.3 also shows the regression within each sub-group for *speeding.* In general, there was some considerable variation across sub-groups in the predictive power of the different measured variables. However, it is necessary to exhibit some caution in interpret-

Table 6.2
Mean Differences Across Groups for Measured Variables (N = 158)

	Driving alone				Same sex passenger				Opposite sex passenger				Group of passengers			
	Males (N=19)		Females (N=20)		Males (N=20)		Females (N=22)		Males (N=20)		Females (N=20)		Males (N=20)		Females (N=17)	
	M	(SD)	M	(SD)	M	(SD)	M	(SD)	M	(SD)	M	(SD)	M	(SD)	M	(SD)
Speeding																
Intention	-.38	(1.46)	.00	(1.61)	-.28	(1.47)	-.01	(1.37)	-.25	(1.47)	-.08	(1.22)	.01	(1.18)	-.81	(1.62)
Behavioural beliefs	-2.72	(1.86)	-2.20	(1.18)	-2.00	(2.56)	-3.17	(1.65)	-2.12	(1.72)	-1.52	(1.94)	-2.05	(1.86)	-2.86	(1.54)
Normative beliefs	-4.21	(4.35)	-5.16	(4.90)	-3.34	(4.54)	-4.39	(4.03)	-2.99	(5.38)	-2.19	(3.32)	-2.54	(5.26)	-5.50	(5.19)
Control beliefs	.93	(2.86)	.59	(3.66)	2.14	(4.31)	-.85	(3.26)	1.22	(2.53)	1.08	(2.40)	1.92	(3.07)	-.04	(3.26)
Anticipated affective reaction	-.16	(1.21)	-1.00	(2.54)	-.30	(2.84)	-.82	(2.30)	-.73	(1.78)	-.43	(1.87)	-.35	(2.08)	-.82	(1.77)
Moral norms	1.11	(1.88)	.40	(1.76)	1.10	(1.74)	.65	(1.72)	.55	(1.50)	.30	(1.53)	.70	(1.84)	.40	(1.90)
Past Behavior	4.83	(1.09)	4.64	(1.24)	4.64	(1.49)	4.71	(1.11)	4.79	(1.43)	4.36	(1.12)	4.28	(1.63)	4.45	(1.10)

Table 6.3
Hierarchical Regressions of Intentions to Speed onto TPB Variables and Additional Variables (Beta Weights and Fit Statistics)

	Overall (N=158)	Driving alone		Same sex passenger		Opposite sex passenger		Group of passengers	
		Males (N=19)	Females (N=20)	Males (N=20)	Females (N=22)	Males (N=20)	Females (N=20)	Males (N=20)	Females (N=17)
Behavioural beliefs	.17**	.01	.24	.33*	.15	.74**	-.36	.05	.24
Normative beliefs	.19**	.60***	-.17	.36*	-.01	-.18	.50	.11	.22
Control beliefs	.19**	.25	.05	-.06	.40	-.07**	.36	.22	.10
Anticipated affective reaction	.12	-.16	.04	.29	.26	-.01	.05	.13	.59*
Moral norms	-.14	-.15	-.60***	-.27	.08	-.15	-.11	-.21	.37
Past behaviour	.36***	.52***	.61**	.37*	.27	.27	.68*	.59	.35
R^2	.45	.80	.83	.77	.32	.68	.66	.52	.59
Model F	20.5***	8.25**	10.9***	7.06**	1.17	4.50*	4.19	2.34	2.40

* $p<0.05$; ** $p0.01$; *** $p0.001$

ing these variations due to the limited number of respondents in any one group. Nevertheless, we did examine differences between the beta weights for males and females within each driving group. Specifically, we performed t-tests to compare the differences in unstandardized beta weights (i.e., the ratio of the difference in unstandardized weights to the standard error of the difference; Edwards, 1984). Given the focus of this paper on social influence, we were particularly interested in differences in the predictive power of normative beliefs. When driving alone, normative beliefs were a significantly stronger predictor of intentions for men than for women ($t(35) = 3.54$, $p<0.0001$). There was no evidence of a difference between men and women for driving with a group of passengers ($t(33) = 0.24$). However, for driving with a single passenger, normative beliefs were stronger predictors when the passenger was male. This difference significant for the opposite sex passenger ($t(36) = 1.88$, $p<0.05$) and non-significant but in the described direction for the same sex passenger ($t(38) = 1.00$).

There were also significant differences for other variables (table 7.3) for *speeding*. When driving with an opposite sex passenger, behavioral beliefs were significantly stronger predictors of intentions for men than for women ($t(36) = 2.99$, $p<0.01$). While, when driving alone, moral norms were significantly stronger predictors of intentions for women than for men ($t(33) = 2.53$, $p<0.01$).

Discussion

This study produced a number of interesting findings. Generally there were few mean differences between males and females in the different conditions on the measured variables in relation to speeding. This is particularly interesting in relation to intentions, where young men compared to young women are usually reported to have stronger intentions to engage in such risky driving behaviors (e.g., Holland & Conner, 1996). The few significant differences observed were, however, based on gender. While both males and females reported social pressure not to speed, this pressure was reported to be greater by women compared to men. Similarly, men compared to women perceived there to be more facilitating than inhibiting factors for speeding and less moral pressure not to speed. Thus young men, compared to young women, appear to perceive greater social pressure and more facilitators towards speeding and less moral norms not to speed.

The multiple regression analysis produced results supportive of the TPB, with intentions being based upon behavioral beliefs, normative beliefs, control beliefs, moral obligations and past behavior (45 percent of variance explained). Unlike Parker et al. (1992b), where normative beliefs were the strongest predictor for intentions, in the present study, past behavior was the strongest predictor for intentions to speed. The direction of effect for control was, however, the same as that reported by Parker et al. (1992b). These data add to the already considerable body of evidence supporting the usefulness of the TPB in understanding the formation of intentions to engage in various behaviors (Ajzen, 1996; Armitage & Conner, 2001). These findings also support the inclusion of additional variables in the TPB (Conner & Armitage, 1998). Similarly, moral norms were a significant independent predictor of intentions to speed. Those who reported moral norms not to perform the behavior were less likely to intend to speed. Again this adds to the existing literature (Conner & Armitage, 1998) supporting the role of moral norms as an independent predictor of intentions for some behaviors. However, the present study did not find support for the role of anticipated affective reaction as an independent predictor of intentions. This is somewhat surprising given the positive findings reported by other studies, including ones on risky driving behaviors (Parker et al., 1995). These data add to the already considerable body of evidence supporting the usefulness of the TPB in understanding the formation of intentions to engage in various behaviors (Ajzen, 1996; Armitage & Conner, 2001). These findings also support the inclusion of additional variables in the TPB. Past behavior showed an independent positive effect on intentions. Those who reported speeding more frequently in the past were more likely to intend to speed. This adds to a growing body of literature supporting the importance of past behavior in the TPB (Conner & Armitage, 1998). Similarly, moral norms not to perform the behavior were less likely to intend to speed. Again this adds to existing literature (Conner & Armitage, 1998) supporting the role of moral norms as an independent predictor of intentions for some behaviors. However, the present study did not find support for the role of anticipated affective reaction as an independent predictor of intentions. This is somewhat surprising given the positive findings reported by other studies, including ones on risky driving behaviors (Parker et al., 1995).

Moderation Effects

Gender and the presence of a passenger also produced a number of interesting moderation effects on the relationships with intentions. Of particular importance in the present study was how the presence of passengers moderated the impact of normative pressure for male and females participants. The young male drivers compared to the young females drivers were more likely to report a greater impact of normative beliefs on their intentions in the driving alone condition. Thus, changing the normative pressure on young males to drive fast when driving alone appears to be a potentially important way to change this behavior. However, such an intervention in women might be less successful.

The patterns of influence in the conditions where one is driving with a passenger were also interesting. In general, respondents reported that normative pressure was a more important determinant of intentions when the passenger was male compared to female (although only some of these differences were significant). This would suggest that changing the perceived normative pressure originating from young men to drive in a risky manner would be a useful way to change risky driving behaviors for both young men and women. It is interesting to note that those who tend to drive in the most risky manner (i.e., young men) are also perceived to be the ones most likely to make others drive in that same way when they are passengers.

There were also difference between males and females when driving with an opposite sex passenger for the impact of behavioral beliefs. In particular, behavioral beliefs were significantly stronger predictors of intentions to speed for men compared to women. Finally, the impact of moral norms varied for men and women when driving alone. In this case, moral norms were significantly stronger predictors of intentions for women compared to men. Thus, in relation to changing intentions to speed it would appear that different strategies are likely to be successful in young male and female drivers. When driving alone, young male drivers are particularly influenced by normative pressure. In contrast, young female drivers are particularly influenced by moral norms not to speed. When driving with others both groups are more influenced by normative pressure when travelling with a male passenger.

Methodological Issues

There are methodological weaknesses worthy of comment in the present research. First, respondents were reacting to hypothetical scenarios. Several authors have commented on the value of using such scenarios in social science research (e.g., Hughes, 1998). However, the potential generalizability of findings based on this methodology has been questioned (Hughes, 1998; Parkinson & Manstead, 1993). Intentions expressed in response to such scenarios may not be translated into action. For example, situational factors may make translation of even strong intentions into actions difficult (Abraham, Sheeran, Abrams, & Spears, 1996; Dockerell & Dockerell, 1992). Nevertheless, reviews of previous research indicate that intentions are generally predictive of a range of behaviors (Armitage & Conner, 2001). Future research might usefully examine the perceived plausibility of such scenarios and the effects on the results. In addition, the use of driving simulators might offer a way to more realistically assess these effects in a safe environment.

Second, the sample sizes in the present study were modest. This lack of power may have limited the significance of a number of the findings. Nevertheless, a number of significant differences were observed. Clearly, we would wish to see the present findings replicated in larger and more representative samples before undue weight is placed upon them.

Conclusions

The present study demonstrates the value of using a scenario approach to understanding normative pressures on intentions to speed. The findings show a number of important influence on the intention to speed. In particular, we note the importance of gender of the passenger in moderating the impact of normative pressure on intentions to engage in this risky driving behavior. The findings provide some interesting insights into the influences on decision-making in relation to risky driving behaviors. The present findings also add to literature demonstrating the effectiveness of the TPB in elucidating the determinants of intentions within the TPB (Ajzen, 1996). In addition, the present findings produced evidence to support past behavior and moral norms as additional predictors of intentions in the TPB (Conner & Armitage, 1998).

References

Abraham, C.S., Sheeran, P., Abrams, D., & Spears, R. (1996). Health beliefs and teenage condom use : A prospective study. *Psychology & Health, 11,* 641-655.

Ajzen, I. (1985). From intentions to action: a theory of planned behaviour. In, J. Kuhl & J. Beckman (Eds.), *Action control: from cognitions to behaviours* (pp.11-39). New York : Springer.

Ajzen, I. (1991). The theory of planned behaviours. *Organizational Behavior and Human Decision Processes, 50,* 179-211.

Bagozzi, R.P., & Kimmel, S.K. (1995). A comparison of leading theories for the prediction of goal-directed behaviours. *British Journal of Social Psychology, 34,* 437-461.

Baxter, J.S., Manstead, A.S.R., Stradling, S.G., Campbell, K.A., Reason, J.T., & Parker, D. (1990). Social facilitation and driver behaviour. *British Journal of Psychology, 81,* 351-360.

Beck, L., & Ajzen, I. (1991). Predicting dishonest actions using the theory of planned behaviour. *Journal of Research in Personality, 25,* 285-301.

Bentler, P.M., & Speckart, G. (1979). Models of attitude-behavior relations. *Psychological Review, 86,* 452-464.

Conner, M., & Armitage, C.J. (1998). Extending the theory of planned behaviour: A review and avenues for further research. *Journal of Applied Social Psychology, 28,* 1430-1464.

Conner, M., & Flesch, D. (2001). Having casual sex: Additive and interactive effects of alcohol and condom availability on the determinants of intentions. *Journal of Applied Social Psychology, 31,* 89-112.

Conner, M., Graham, S., & Moore, B. (1999). Alcohol and intentions to use condoms: Applying the theory of planned behaviour. *Psychology and Health, 14,* 795-812.

Conner, M., & Sparks, P. (1996). The theory of planned behaviour and health behaviours. In, M. Conner & P. Norman (Eds.), *Predicting health behaviour* (pp.121-162). Buckingham, UK : Open University Press.

Conner, M., Warren, R., Close, S., & Sparks, P. (1999). Alcohol consumption and the theory of planned behaviour : An examination of the cognitive mediation of past behaviour. *Journal of Applied Social Psychology, 29,* 1675-1703.

Dockerell, J.E., & Dockerell, W.B. (1992). An analyses of theoretical models for HIV/ AIDS education. Poster presented at the *XXV International Congress of Psychology,* 19-24 July, Brussels.

Eagly, A.L. (1984). *An introduction to linear regression and correlation (*2nd edition).New York : Freeman.

Godin, G., Valois, P., & Lepage, L. (1993). The pattern of influence of perceived behavioural control upon exercising behaviour – an application of Ajzen's theory of planned behaviour. *Journal of Behavioral Medicine, 16,* 81-102.

Harre, N., Field, J., & Kirkwood, B. (1996). Gender differences and areas of common concern in the driving behaviours and attitudes of adolescents. *Journal of Safety Research, 27,* 163-173.

Holland, C.A., & Conner, M.T. (1996). Speeding behaviour and attitudes: an evaluation of the effectiveness of a police intervention. *Accident Analysis and Prevention, 28,* 587-597.

Hughes, R. (1998). Considering the vignette technique and its application to study of drug injecting and HIV risk and safer behaviour. *Sociology of Health and Illness, 20,* 381-400.

Leigh, B.C., Aramburu, B., & Norris, J. (1992). The morning after – Gender differences in attributions about alcohol-related sexual encounters. *Journal of Applied Social Psychology, 22,* 343-357.

Manstead, A.S.R (1999). The role of moral norm in the attitude-behavior relationship. In, D.J. Terry, & M.A. Hogg (Eds.), *Attitudes, behaviour and social context : The role of norms and group membership.* Mahwah, NJ: Lawrence Erlbaum

Norman, P., & Smith, L. (1995). The theory of planned behaviour and exercise: An investigation into the role of prior behaviour, behavioural intentions and attitude variability. *European Journal of Social Psychology, 25,* 403-415.

Parker, D., Manstead, A.S.R., & Stradling, S.G. (1995). Extending the theory of planned behaviour: The role of personal norm. *British Journal of Social Psychology, 34,* 127-137.

Parker, D., Manstead, A.S.R., Stradling, S.G., Reason, J.T., & Baxter, J.S. (1992b). Intention to commit driving violations – an application of the theory of planned behavior. *Journal of Applied Psychology, 77,* 94-101.

Parker, D., Stradling, S.G., & Manstead, A.S.R. (1996). Modifying beliefs and attitudes to exceeding the speed limit: An intervention study based on the theory of planned behaviour. *Journal of Applied Social Psychology, 26,* 1-19.

Parkinson, B., & Manstead, A.S.R. (1993). Making sense of emotion in stories and social life. *Cognition and Emotion, 7,* 295-323.

Richard, R., Van der Pligt, J., & de Vries, N. (1996a). Affective reactions and time perspective: Changing sexual risk-taking behaviour. *Journal of Behavioural Decision Making, 9,* 185-199.

Sheppard, B.H., Hartwick, J., & Warshaw, P.R. (1988). The theory of reasoned action: A meta-analysis of past research with recommendations for modifications and future research. *Journal of Consumer Research, 15,* 325-343.

Sparks, P., Shepherd, R., & Frewer, L.J. (1995). Assessing and structuring attitudes toward the use of gene technology in food production: The role of perceived ethical obligation. *Basic and Applied Social Psychology, 16,* 267-285.

Sutton, S. (1994). The past predicts the future: Interpreting behaviour-behaviour relationships in social psychological models of health behaviour. In, D. R. Rutter & L. Quine (Eds.), *Social psychology and health: European perspectives* (pp. 71-88). Aldershot, UK: Avebury.

7

Implications of Goal Theories for the Theories of Reasoned Action and Planned Behavior

Charles Abraham and Paschal Sheeran

In his presidential address to the first annual meeting of the American Psychological Association, Division of Personality and Social Psychology, Allport (1947) insisted that it was "necessary" for psychologists to adopt of "the concept of 'intention.'" Contrasting intentions with drives and instincts, he recommended that psychologists study "private worlds of desire, aspiration, and conscience" (p.186) and acknowledge the role of longer-term goals in directing and make sense of everyday action. He proposed that current goals are best understood as the means by which longer-term goals are realized; "the specific goals we set for ourselves are almost always subsidiary to our long range intentions. A good parent, a good neighbour, a good citizen is not good because his [*sic*] specific goals are acceptable but because his successive goals are ordered to a dependable and socially desirable set of values" (p. 188). In the present paper, we contend that Allport's insights concerning the relations between longer-term goals, on the one hand, and intentions to perform specific behaviors, on the other, is overlooked by the dominant accounts of cognition-behavior relations—the theory of reasoned action (Fishbein, 1967; 1980; Fishbein & Ajzen, 1975) and the theory of planned behavior (TPB; Ajzen, 1985; 1991). We argue that these theories should be augmented to take account of insights from goal theories and we make several suggestions about how this development might be achieved.

The Theories of Reasoned Action and Planned Behavior

The TPB is an extension of Fishbein and Ajzen's theory of reasoned action (TRA) that was designed to permit accurate prediction of behaviors that present problems of volitional control (Ajzen, 1991). Like the TRA, the TPB proposes; (a) that the best predictor of behavior is the person's *intention* or decision to perform it (e.g., "I intend to do X"), (b) that intentions are determined by people's evaluations of performing behavior (*attitude*; e.g., "Doing X would be good/bad") and by their perceptions of social pressure to perform it (*subjective norm*; "People who are important to me think that I should do X"), and (c) that external variables (variables not contained in the model) only have indirect effects on behavior—these variables either moderate, or their effects are mediated by, components of the model. The TPB extends the TRA by including one additional construct—*perceived behavioral control* (PBC). PBC is derived from Bandura's (1977, 1997) concept of self-efficacy (Ajzen, 1998) and refers to people's appraisals of their ability to perform a behavior (e.g., "Doing X would be easy/difficult"). PBC is conceived as a determinant of intention (because people are unlikely to intend to do impossible things) and behavior (when perceptions of control accurately reflect actual control over the behavior).

The TPB has received considerable support in correlational surveys. Meta-analyses indicate that attitude, subjective norm, and PBC explain 30-50 percent of the variance in intention (Armitage & Conner, 2001; Sheeran & Taylor, 1999) and that intention and PBC explain 20-40 percent of the variance in behavior (Armitage & Conner, 2001; Godin & Kok, 1996; Sheeran & Orbell, 1998). The TPB possesses two particular strengths. First, the model is parsimonious; only a small number of variables need to be measured in order to obtain accurate prediction of behavior. Second, the TPB provides clear guidelines about how to measure cognitions specified by the model, in order to ensure predictive accuracy (Ajzen & Fishbein, 1980). For example, the TPB highlights the importance of ensuring that measures of attitude, subjective norm, PBC, intention, and behavior are compatible (i.e., all refer to the same action, target, context, and time), and are taken as closely as possible in time. Thus, as a model of the cognitive antecedents of behavior, the TPB is parsimonious, empirically supported and can be operationalized easily, according to available guidelines

Goal Theories

A comprehensive review of goal theories is beyond the scope of this paper (see Austin & Vancouver, 1996; Gollwitzer & Moskowitz, 1996, for extensive reviews). We shall restrict our discussion of this literature to defining goals and describing a small number of propositions espoused by most goal theorists. According to Austin and Vancouver (1996), goals are "internally desired states where states are broadly construed as outcomes, events or processes" (p.338). People have multiple goals that are related to one another: "single goals cannot be understood when isolated from other goals and from the cognitive, behavioral and affective responses organized in pursuing goals" (p.338). Of course, not all goals are equally important (cf. Ryan, Sheldon, Kasser, & Deci, 1996). Most theorists agree that goals are hierarchically organized with abstract higher-order goals being translated into lower-level goals that ultimately direct muscle movements (e.g., Miller, Galanter, & Pribraum, 1960; Carver & Scheier 1982; 1998; Hyland, 1998; Karoly, 1985; Powers, 1973). For example, Carver and Scheier's (1998) control theory places self-related goals or *system concepts* (e.g., "be a successful person") at the top of the hierarchy, abstract action goals (*principles*; e.g., "work hard at my job") in the middle, and courses of action (*programs*; e.g., "stay working the office after 5PM") at the bottom.

Hierarchical organization of goals has two important implications. First, goal hierarchies imply action *sequences*—achieving one or more sub-goals may be necessary before the broader goal can be achieved. Bagozzi (1992) noted that achieving our goals often requires us to undertake preparatory or "instrumental" actions. For example, staying late at work may be required to achieve one's goal of working hard and working hard, in turn, may be required in order to achieve the goal of being a successful person. However, even the sub-goal of staying late at work may involve further sub-goals such as arranging child care, cancelling drinks with friends, or bringing food to work stave off hunger. Consequently, goal achievement may require considerable action planning. A second implication of goal hierarchies is the potential for conflict between goals. Goal conflict occurs when more than one goal cannot simultaneously be attained (Carver & Scheier, 1998). For example, the goal of being a successful person may conflict with the goal of intimacy with one's partner and the person may need to prioritize or reschedule one of these goals (see

Dodge, Asher, & Pankhurst, 1989). The importance of planning action sequences and resolving goal conflict to goal attainment was highlighted by Karoly (1998) who identified "goal imprecision" and "intergoal conflict" as the "twin demons" of action regulation.

Why, then are some goals prioritized over others? Research on action identification theory (Vallacher & Wegner, 1985; 1987) has shown that the situational context can alter the salience of particular goals. For example, if one receives feedback that one's job performance is poorer than expected, then the goal of being a successful person is likely to be more salient than the goal of spending time with one's partner. Conversely, the arrival of one's anniversary is likely to make intimacy with one's partner more salient compared to being a successful person. The situational context can also alter which goal is salient or prepotent in relation to a particular behavior. For example, staying late at work could be related to the goal of being a successful person or—if one's relationship was going badly—it might be related to the goal of avoiding conflict with one's partner. In summary, most goal theories consider multiple and hierarchically organized goals that imply sequences of sub-goals and incorporate the potential for goal conflict. Moreover, contextual factors may determine what goal is salient at any particular moment.

Goals and the Theory of Planned Behavior

Ajzen and Fishbein (1969) demonstrated how the theory of reasoned action could be adapted to consider alternative goals by examining the cognitive antecedents of eight alternative things to do "on a Friday night," including "going to a concert," "playing poker," "watching a French movie," "going to a party," and "visiting an exhibition of modern art." In this study respondents rank ordered the eight activities according how likely they, personally, were to do each on a Friday night and also completed twenty-eight bipolar response scales indicating whether they were more likely to do one than another. In general, however, the TRA and TPB have been applied to single behaviors (e.g., people's intentions to exercise four times in the next two weeks, cf. Abraham & Sheeran, in press) and treatment of goals has been limited to consideration of measurement issues relevant to the prediction of goals (or "outcomes") versus behaviors (Ajzen & Fishbein, 1980; Fishbein, 1980).

Fishbein (1980) described the example of the "goal intention" of trying to lose weight. This goal intention is contingent upon the performance of behaviors—exercise and diet in this case. As figure 7.1 illustrates perceived control in relation to the goal (goal PBC), predicts goal intention which, in turn, predict behavioral intentions that, in combination with PBC for that behavior, predicts the relevant behavior (see too Bagozzi & Edwards, 1998). However, external factors such as metabolic rate can influence the extent to which exercise and dieting behaviors affect weight loss and can also have direct effects on goal achievement. Thus, for the TRA/TPB, goals are important because intention-behavior relations do not adequately account for goal achievement. This is supported by a meta-analysis of TRA applications showing that intentions are significantly better predictors of behaviors, than they are of goal achievement (Sheppard, Hartwick, and Warshaw, 1988; rs = .58 and .45, respectively).

Figure 7.1
TRA/TPB Analysis of the Relationship Between Goal Intentions, Behavioral Intentions, Behavior, and Goal Achievement

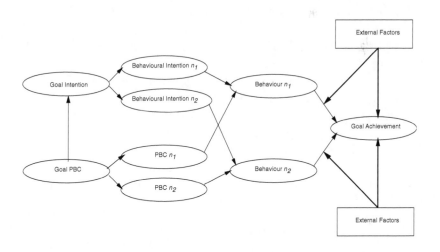

Focusing on the prediction of single behaviors obscures the relationship of that behavior (e.g., exercising) to other actions the person may undertake in pursuit of the same goal (e.g., eating a healthy diet) or in pursuit of potentially competing goals (e.g., staying late at work or going out to dinner). Consequently, the TPB cannot explain evidence indicating that the performance of health-promoting behaviors such as healthy eating and exercising are positively correlated with one another, and are negatively correlated with health-risk behaviors such as smoking and excessive drinking (e.g., Belloc & Breslow, 1972). The TPB offers predictive accuracy about particular things people do—but at the expense of perspective on what binds together the variety of things that people do.

Acknowledging that people's intentions to perform specific behaviors are based, at least partly, upon their broad goals (Eagly & Chaiken, 1993; Sheeran & Trafimow, 2001), makes sense of positive correlations between exercise and healthy eating and negative relations between exercise and smoking because *being healthy* is an important goal for many people. Similarly, the negative relationship between "attending all of one's lectures in the next two weeks" and "going to the pub four times" and "going clubbing twice" in the same time period, is observed because academic success and socialising are conflicting goals (Sheeran, Norman & Orbell, 1999). Sheeran (2001) showed that participants primed with achievement goals intended to study more than they intended to socialise over the next forty-eight hours whereas participants primed with the affiliation goals intended to socialise more than they intended to study over the same period. Thus viewing specific behaviors as serving longer-term goals helps us understand how different behaviors performed by the same person relate to one another.

Conceptualization of behavior in relation to goal hierarchies has implications for various aspects of the TPB and, in the sections that follow, we illustrate how goal theory can inform the TPB. We also make suggestions about self-report measures and computational procedures that might improve prediction and understanding of particular behaviors.

Behavioral Selection

The TRA/TPB addresses the question of whether or not a person will perform a behavior. As Fishbein (1980) stated: "The ultimate goal of the theory is to predict and understand an individual's behavior. The first step towards this goal is to identify and measure the behavior of interest" (p. 66). In contrast, the starting point for goal theorists is that people must decide what behaviors should be performed in order to achieve their goals. Thus, for the TRA/TPB, the focal behavior has already been selected (usually by the researcher) whereas for goal theorists, how and why a particular behavior is selected are key research questions. From a goal theory perspective, there is always a choice about what action should be undertaken to achieve one's goal *and* what goal one should pursue at any particular time. If one is prevented from pursuing a particular course of action then a different behavior (in pursuit of the goal) must be identified, or, alternatively, a different goal prioritized.

Discussion of the TRA/TPB has been equivocal about behavioral selection. It has been suggested that consideration of cognitions referring to alternative behaviors is unnecessary because these cognitions will only affect a focal behavior through their effects on behavior-specific attitude, subjective norm, PBC, and intention, that is, measures of cognitions about alternative behaviors are superlative (see Fishbein & Ajzen, 1975). However, as we have noted above, other TRA/TPB-based models (such as Ajzen & Fishbien, 1969) acknowledge that people make choices between behavioral alternatives—at least in some contexts. For example, Sperber, Fishbein, and Ajzen (1980) and Fishbein, Ajzen, and Hinkle (1980) (in studies of women's occupational decisions [i.e., pursuing a career versus home-making] and voting behavior, respectively) obtained separate measures of attitude, subjective norm, and intention for two behavioral alternatives. The researchers then computed *differential* measures of each construct by subtracting scores on one alternative from scores on the other. Findings indicated that the differential measures provided better prediction of intention and behavior compared to measures that referred to a single alternative.

Although differential measures of the TRA/TPB constructs seem to be able represent the process of behavioral selection, they have some limitations. Measures based on difference possess inherent ambiguities because participants can arrive at the same difference score even though their scores on the original measures are radically different (see Edwards, 1994; Griffin, Murray, & Gonzalez, 1999, for reviews). Griffin et al. (1999) outlined statistical procedures to overcome this problem, though their recommendations are rather complex. A different measurement strategy would be to conduct within-participants analyses of alternative behaviors and assign a score of "1" to the highest attitude/subjective norm/PBC/intention scores and "0" to the alternatives. Davidson and Morrison (1983) demonstrated that this procedure had greater predictive validity than traditional between-participants analyses in relation to contraceptive choice. A difficulty with this procedure is that a lot of data may be lost due to score ties (e.g., attitudes towards more than one alternative are both "7" on 1-7 scales). Two more practical possibilities are: (a) participants rank order their attitudes, etc. in relation to the behavioral alternatives (cf. Ajzen & Fishbein, 1969); the rank data could then be transformed to Z-scores to permit parametric statistical analyses, or (b) participants provide comparative ratings of behavioral alternatives on a single scale. A sample item contrasting two alternative actions might be:

Which contraceptive method would more convenient for you to use next time you have sex?

Condom much more convenient:—:—:—:—:—:—:—:*Pill much more convenient*

These procedures may appear to be applicable only in contexts where the choice between behavioral alternatives is fairly obvious (e.g., contraceptive and consumer decisions, voting choice). However, we believe that the prediction even of putative "single actions" such as exercise or playing the lottery are likely to benefit from measures that capture the process of behavioral selection. Of course, deciding what behavioral alternatives should be included in a questionnaire may be more difficult for single actions. However, pilot research (which could be conducted alongside the elicitation of modal salient beliefs, cf. Ajzen & Fishbein, 1980) should allow researchers to identify behaviors commonly complement, conflict with, or represent a different route to a particular goal.

Sheppard et al's (1988) meta-analysis supports the view that measures reflecting the behavioral selection process inherent to goal achievement are likely to enhance the prediction of specific behaviors. These researchers compared the predictive capacity of the theory of reasoned action when operationalized in terms of (i) behavior choice, or relative likelihood of a behavior and (ii) the likelihood of a single behavior (without consideration of alternatives). They found that when a choice between behavioral alternatives was specified attitude and subjective norm better predicted intention (multiple rs = .80 vs. .67) and intention better predicted behavior (rs =.72 vs. .42, respectively). These data cannot be explained by the TRA/TPB but are predictable when behavioral selection is considered. They suggest that focusing respondents' attention on behavioral choice when measuring cognitions results in more accurate anticipation of the decisions that direct future action.

Goal Imprecision and Planning

The sequential nature of goal-directed behavior implies that people plan their actions. Consequently, the extent to which a goal has been translated into specific action plans is likely to determine how easily it can be achieved. Stock and Cervone (1990) have shown that subdividing a complex task into a series of sub-goals leads to higher confidence of success at task outset and at sub-task completion. Thus, perceived behavioral control may be partly determined by the extent to which people have planned or envisaged goal enactment routes in terms of sequences of sub-goals. Stock and Cervone (1990) also report that sub-goal planning led to enhanced persistence, highlighting one mechanism by which planning may affect performance.

Gollwitzer and colleagues (1993; Gollwitzer & Brandstatter, 1997; Gollwitzer & Oettingen, 1998) have shown that intentions are more likely to be enacted if they are translated into "implementation intentions," that is, plans specifying when and where a particular action is to be undertaken (see Gollwitzer & Schaal, 1998; Sheeran, 2002, for reviews). Gollwitzer's studies have shown that those who have formed implementation intentions are better able to recall presented descriptions of the means to carry out an action, more likely to identify environmental cues relevant to their planned action, and faster to initiate action in response to situational opportunities. This body of research suggests that specific action planning results in automatic goal prioritization in response to contextual cues represented in prior plans. It also implies that the extent to which a person has planned how (s)he will perform a behavior is predictive of successful enactment.

Researchers have developed measures of the degree to which respondents' have planned how to perform a behavior. Abraham et al. (1999) used self-report measures to assess the extent to which people had thought about, or developed a clear plan, in relation to the negotiation of condom use with a partner. This measure was highly correlated with a discriminant function capable of distinguishing between intenders who did or did not use a condom. Similar measures of planning were employed by Jones, Abraham, Harris, Schulz, and Chrispin (2001) who found that they enhanced the prediction of sun screen use after the effects of intention were controlled. Moreover, in this study, almost half of the total effect of intention measures on behavior was mediated by planning and there was no evidence of a reciprocal relationship between planning and intention. These findings suggest that self-report measures of planning could enhance the TPB and help to explain how intentions are translated into action.

Goal Conflict and Intention-Behavior Consistency

People often fail to act upon their intentions. For example, Sheeran (2002) found that the median percentage of participants who failed to enact their intentions to engage in various health behaviors was 47. So why is there such a large gap between intentions and behavior? When participants are asked why they failed to act, they generally say "I forgot," "I didn't get round to it," or "I was too busy" (see Milne, Orbell, & Sheeran, in press; Orbell, Hodgkins, & Sheeran, 1998). In our view, such statements are often markers for goal conflict. People forget to act, do not get round to it, or are busy because they are pursuing other goals that are at odds with performance of the focal behavior. For example, people may fail to use a condom because they want to have unprotected sex; students may not study because they want to socialize instead; we stay up late despite having to work the next day because our friendships are more important, at the time, than is our career.

The TRA/TPB explains intention-behavior discrepancies in two ways. The person did not have control over performing the behavior so her intention could not be translated into action, or the person received new attitudinal, normative, or control information and changed her intention to perform the behavior (Ajzen, 1985). According to Ajzen (1985) an ideal measure of intention, in TRA/TPB terms, "must reflect respondents' intentions as they exist just prior to the performance of the behavior," p.18). If such measures were available, then we would expect very small discrepancies between intentions and behaviors. However, accepting this condition as necessary for accurate prediction of behavior by intention risks triviality because researchers are rarely in a position to measure intention immediately prior to enactment. In practice we require self-report measures that predict the likelihood of behavior (often well) in advance of the actual opportunity to act.

So can goal theories offer self-report measures that index potential goal conflict in advance of the action? Available evidence suggests they can. Abraham et al. (1999) examined whether goal conflict could explain discrepancies between intentions to use a condom and subsequent condom use. They hypothesized that participants who prioritise the goal of having sex over the goal of protecting oneself against HIV would be more likely to abandon their intention to use a condom (because insisting on using a condom could threaten the likelihood of having sex, cf. Wight, 1992). The questionnaire measure used the stem, "Thinking about the hours before you had vaginal intercourse for the first time with this person"; respondents were asked "How important to you was (i) having vaginal intercourse with him/her and (ii) using a condom if you had vaginal intercourse" to measure the importance of the two goals. Abraham et al. then computed a measure of the relative importance of having sex vs. having sex using a condom and examined whether this measure could distinguish between participants who intended to use a condom and subsequently used one versus participants who intended to use a condom but did not use one. Findings showed that the relative importance of condom use was the strongest predictor of intention-behavior discrepancies—even when several planning and self-efficacy measures were included as predictors. These findings suggest that relative goal importance provides information about actors' goal structures that is not represented by single-behavior intention measures and that such measures can help understand intention-behavior discrepancies. In other words, making multiple goals (relevant to the likelihood of a behavior) salient at the point of measurement can facilitate more accurate prediction of decision making *in situ*.

Goal Conflict and the Dynamics of Behavioral Selection

Similar reasoning—and measures—can also be used to examine how people "change their minds" about performing particular behaviors, and how the situational context can prompt such cognition change. Sheeran and Trafimow (2001) investigated the role of goal conflict in choosing different contraceptive methods at different stages of a relationship. As part of the research, participants were asked "How big an influence" two goals would have on their choice of contraceptive method at five points in a relationship, one month, six months, one year, two years, and five years. The goals were preventing sexually transmitted diseases (STDs) and maintaining sexual spontaneity. Findings showed that the salience of maintaining sexual spontaneity increased significantly at each time-point (up to two years) whereas the salience of STD prevention declined significantly over time. Sheeran and Trafimow also measured intentions to use a condom and intentions to use the contraceptive pill at each time point. Intentions to use condoms declined significantly at each succeeding time-point whereas intentions to use the contraceptive pill increased over time. One month into the relationship, intentions to use condoms were significantly stronger than intentions to use the pill but, at one year, intentions to use the pill were significantly stronger than were intentions to use condoms. As figure 7.2 indicates, the decline in the salience of the STD prevention goal over time was paralleled by reduced intentions to use condoms, whereas the increasing salience of the sexual spontaneity goal was paralleled by stronger intentions to use the contraceptive pill. These findings underline the utility of assessing the goals underlying behavioral intentions in order to understand how people's choices change over time.

Sheeran and Trafimow (2001) also demonstrated how the salience of particular goals can be altered by immediate features of the environment. In a second study, they manipulated whether the title of the study questionnaire was "Attitudes towards HIV/AIDS" or "Attitudes towards methods of contraception." Participants were asked to imagine that they had been having a sexual relationship with someone for about a year and were asked how likely it was that they would intend to use a condom during sex with that person. Participants were subsequently asked to rate the extent to which HIV/AIDS prevention versus pregnancy prevention goals had occurred to them

Figure 7.2

Changes in Goal Salience and Behavioral Intentions Over the Course of a Sexual Relationship (Adapted from Sheeran & Trafimow, 2001)

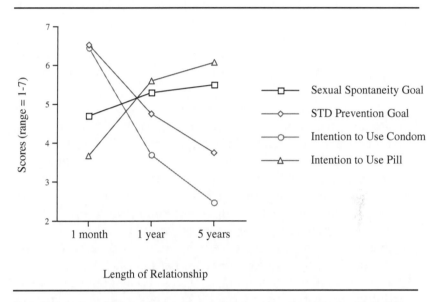

Note. Higher scores indicate greater salience of goals and stronger behavioral intentions.

(i.e., the extent to which they "thought of this" or "did not think of this"). Participants who completed the "HIV/AIDS" questionnaire had stronger intentions to use a condom compared to participants who completed the "contraception" questionnaire. The manipulation also affected the salience of the two goals; completing the HIV/AIDS questionnaire meant that participants were more likely to have thought about HIV/AIDS prevention whereas completing the contraception questionnaire meant that participants were more likely to have thought about pregnancy prevention.

A final experiment used a subliminal priming paradigm to make the goal of STD prevention salient for one group of participants. Compared to a no-prime control group, participants primed with STD prevention intended to use condoms for a longer period during their sexual relationships (values were six weeks vs. forty-four weeks). These findings suggest that it is possible to demonstrate empirically how situational contexts can alter the goals that are salient and, thereby, change behavioral intentions.

Operationalizing Goal Prioritization

Demonstrations that varying the title of a questionnaire title or priming participants with goals outside their conscious awareness (cf. Dijksterhuis & Bargh, 2001) might appear to threaten the predictive validity of behavioral intention. If people are exposed to a variety of stimuli that alter the salience of different goals, how do they manage to enact particular intentions? Why do some people exhibit strong intention-behavior consistency whereas other people do not? More importantly, can we measure the likelihood that people will maintain the priority of particular goals and intentions?

In our view, the degree of prioritization of particular intentions and the extent to which intentions are shielded from conflicting goals (cf. Kuhl, 1985; 1992) can be operationalized by measures of the temporal stability of intention and/or PBC. It is worth noting that temporal stability of intention/PBC is not equivalent to Fishbein and Ajzen's recommendation that intention be measured as closely as possible to the performance of the behavior. This is because temporal stability is a *property* of intention; the fact that an intention is stable or unstable does not bring the measure any closer to the moment of the behavioral performance. Sheeran and Abraham (in press) demonstrated that more stable intentions were associated with a variety of goal-relevant constructs such as basing the intention on one's personal beliefs rather than social pressure and the centrality of the focal behavior to one's self-definition.

Intention stability has characteristically been measured by within-participants correlations between measures of intention taken at two time-points (e.g., Sheeran, Orbell, & Trafimow, 1999). However, when there are too few intention items to compute within-participants correlations, other indices can be used, including the absolute difference between the sum of intention items and the number of items that exhibit change (see Conner, Sheeran, Norman, & Armitage, 2000). Evidence indicates that temporal stability is a powerful moderator of intention-behavior consistency. For example, Sheeran et al. (1999) showed that when intentions were stable, participants' behavior was strongly determined by their intentions, and past behavior was not a significant predictor. In contrast, when intentions were unstable, intention did not predict behavior, and past behavior was the most powerful predictor (see also Conner et al., 2000). Moreover, a recent meta-analysis showed that temporal stability was the most powerful moderator of the intention-behavior relationship when compared to six other properties of intention (Cooke & Sheeran, 2001). These findings are particularly interesting in the light of recent analysis of the past behavior-future behavior relation as a form of goal-directed automaticity (Aarts & Dijksterhuis, 2000; Verplanken & Aarts, 2000). According to this view, habits are behaviors that are (or were) functional in terms of achieving particular goals and strong associations have developed between particular environmental cues and particular action schemas. The difficulty, of course, is that some habits (e.g., smoking) may be contrary to the person's current goals. Findings showing that stable intentions attenuate the effects of habit suggests that intention stability can be used to measure to what extent the person prioritises their current goals (e.g., not smoking) over the goals associated with the habitual behavior.

Implications of the Content of Goals

The TPB specifies three types of beliefs that are presumed to underlie attitude, subjective norm, and perceived behavioral control, namely, behavioral, normative, and control beliefs, respectively. According to the TPB, further distinctions between different kinds of beliefs (e.g., moral norms) are not necessary because these other belief types are likely to predict only a limited range of behaviors (e.g., behaviors that involve an ethical component). Considerable research has been devoted to consideration of "additional variables" that might be used to augment the TPB, that we will not review here (see Abraham, Sheeran, & Johnson, 1998; Conner & Armitage, 1998). Several goal theories are concerned with the *content* of people's goals, and with the implications of different goal content for the likelihood of performance. This has further implications for the TRA/ TPB.

Consider the example of two people, Jenny and Rachel, who intend to exercise. Let us say that Jenny believes that exercising is "very likely to improve health and well-being," has a very positive evaluation of "improving health and well-being," and rates this belief about health and well-being as the most important belief underlying her attitude (cf. van der Pligt, de Vries, Manstead, & van Harreveld, 2000). Rachel, on the other hand, believes that exercising is "very likely to increase sexual attractiveness," has a very positive evaluation of "increasing sexual attractiveness," and rates this as her most important belief (see Bagozzi and Edwards, 1998 for an empirical exploration of goal structures underlying weight loss). Let us also assume that Jenny and Rachel have a similar overall attitude toward exercise when all of their behavioral beliefs are multiplied by outcome evaluations and weighted by belief importance. According to the TRA/TPB, Jenny and Rachel will have equivalent likelihood of engaging in exercise behavior because their attitudes are the same. However, according to self-determination theory (e.g., Deci & Ryan, 1985; Ryan & Connell, 1989; Ryan et al., 1996), Jenny should be much more likely to exercise compared to Rachel. This is because Jenny is motivated by beliefs associated with an *intrinsic* goal (i.e., her personal health and well-being) whereas Rachel is motivated by beliefs associated with an *extrinsic* goal (i.e., a goal associated with external agents, in this case, how one appears to other people); considerable research indicates that goal achievement is much more likely when people are intrinsically motivated compared to when people are extrinsically motivated (e.g., Deci & Ryan, 1985).

The TRA/TPB is not concerned with the content of people's beliefs (beyond ensuring that modal salient attitudinal, normative, and control beliefs are presented to participants, cf. Ajzen & Fishbein, 1980). For goal theories, however, the contents of beliefs, evaluations, and importance ratings is crucial because these contents indicate whether the goals underlying people's decisions are intrinsic or extrinsic which, in turn, is likely to determine whether or not the decision leads to action. This analysis suggests that researchers might do well to code behavioral beliefs in terms of their goal contents, e.g., in terms of intrinsic versus extrinsic goals (Deci & Ryan, 1985), higher- versus lower-level identifications (Vallacher & Wegner, 1985; 1987), or presence vs. absence of system concepts (Carver & Scheier, 1998). If the researcher has obtained ratings of belief importance, then it would be a relatively simple matter to characterise participants in terms of particular goal content underlying their attitudes, and to investigate the impact of these characterizations on cognition-intention, and intention-behavior, relations.

In cases where belief importance ratings are not available, then it should be feasible to determine the degree of match between attitude and each behavioral belief multiplied by its evaluation. For example, if attitude, beliefs, and evaluations are all measured on 1-

7 scales, dividing each belief X evaluation score by 7 will ensure that belief X evaluation scores are on a similar metric as attitude scores (i.e., both range from 1 to 7). One could then use the absolute difference between attitude scores and belief X evaluation scores to identify which belief X evaluation score most closely matches the participant's attitude score—and thereby identify the key belief underlying the attitude. For each participant, one then simply has to code the goal content associated with the belief X evaluation score that most closely matches his/her attitude score for use in subsequent analyses. This type of analysis would permit a fine-grained depiction of the goals underlying each participant's attitude/intention and is likely to enhance the prediction of his/her behavior.

Similar reasoning extends to the relative weight attached to attitude, subjective norm, and perceived behavioral control in forming a behavioral intention. According to the TRA/TPB, the weight attached to these different determinants of intention varies according to the behavior being studied; the relative weights do not themselves matter—what matters is the participant's intention score. However, self-determination theory suggests that the weight attached to different determinants of intention has important motivational consequences. This is because self-determination theory distinguishes between two types of motivation; autonomous and controlled. Autonomous motivation involves intentions that are experienced as self-chosen and emanating from self whereas controlled motivation involves intentions that are initiated and pursued because of external factors (such as social pressure from significant others). According to self-determination theory, goal achievement is more likely when people's motivation is autonomous compared to when motivation is controlled (e.g., Chatzisarantis, Biddle, & Meek, 1997; Sheldon & Elliott, 1998; Williams, Grow, Friedman, Ryan, & Deci, 1996). Sheeran, Norman, and Orbell (1999) suggested that the distinction between autonomous versus controlled motivation corresponds to a distinction between attitudinal versus normative control of intention (cf. Trafimow & Finlay, 1996), i.e., whether people's intentions are more strongly determined by their attitude or by their subjective norm. If self-determination theory is accurate, then attitudinally controlled participants should show stronger intention-behavior consistency compared to normatively controlled participants.

Sheeran et al. (1999) tested this idea in a study of thirty behaviors that used the relative strength of the within-participants correlations between attitude and intention versus subjective norm and intention to designate participants as "attitudinally" and "normatively controlled." More recently, Sheeran and Abraham (in press) used a simpler calculation to achieve the same designation. This involved computing the absolute difference between intention and attitude scores and between intention and subjective norm scores for each participant, and using the value that represented the smaller discrepancy to characterise participants as attitudinally versus normatively controlled. Importantly, support was obtained for the prediction from self-determination theory, regardless of how attitudinal versus normative control was calculated: Both studies showed that attitudinally controlled intentions were more likely to be enacted than were normatively controlled intentions. Sheeran and Abraham (in press) also showed attitudinal versus normative control moderated the intention-behavior relation because attitudinal control was associated with greater stability of intention—basing one's decision on one's personal beliefs (rather than social pressure to perform the behavior) was associated with greater prioritization of the focal intention. In summary, goal content theories suggest that research on the TRA/TPB would benefit from close analyses of the goals that underlie intention since evidence suggests that the quality of people's motivation can be quite different—despite equivalent intention scores.

Conclusion

We have argued that ideas derived from goal theories can enhance the level of prediction and understanding provided by the TRA/TPP theories of reasoned action and planned behavior. Our analysis of goal theories suggests that: (a) behaviors are selected by people in order to achieve their goals, (b) the extent to which people have planned how they will undertake a behavior or action sequence is predictive of performance (c) goal conflict is an important source of discrepancies between intentions and behavior, (d) contextual factors can alter the salience of particular goals which, in turn, give rise to predictable changes in people's behavioral choices, (e) the temporal stability of intention provides a useful indicator of goal prioritization, and (f) it is useful to categorise the beliefs underlying TRA/TPB in terms of their goal contents. We have also made suggestions concerning the types of self-report measures and computations that would permit greater use of ideas from goal theories in studies applying the TRA/TPB.

We readily acknowledge that our presentation of goal theories is highly selective and represents only a partial overview of this literature. For example, we have not discussed the potential of goal-setting interventions in promoting behavioral performance (see Locke, Shaw, Saari, Latham, 1981; Tubbs, 1986, for reviews). Nevertheless, our analysis has highlighted the theoretical and practical importance of Allport's (1947) insights into the role of longer-term goals in directing everyday behavior. The implications of these arguments are clear. Developing measures of cognition derived from goal theories and integrating these with the measures stipulated by the TRA/TPB will provide better models of the cognitive antecedents of action and more accurate prediction of behavior.

References

Aarts, H., & Dijksterhuis, A. (2000). Habits as knowledge structure: automaticity in goal-directed behavior. *Journal of Personality and Social Psychology, 78*, 53-63.

Abraham, C., & Sheeran, P. (in press). Acting on intentions: The role of anticipated regret. *British Journal of Social Psychology.*

Abraham, C., Sheeran, P., & Johnson, M. (1998) From health beliefs to self-regulation: Theoretical advances in the psychology of action control. *Psychology and Health, 13,* 569-592.

Abraham, C., Sheeran, P., Norman, P., Conner, M., de Vries, N., & Otten, W. (1999) When good intentions are not enough: Modeling post-intention cognitive correlates of condom use. *Journal of Applied Social Psychology, 29,* 2591-2612.

Allport, G., W. (1947). Scientific models and human morals. *Psychological Review, 54,* 182-192.

Ajzen, I. (1985). From intentions to actions: A theory of planned behavior. In J. Kuhl & J. Beckmann (Eds.), *Action control: From cognition to behavior* (pp. 11-39). Berlin: Springer-Verlag.

Ajzen, I. (1991). The theory of planned behavior. *Organizational Behavior and Human Decision Processes, 50,* 179-211.

Ajzen, I. (1998). Models of human social behavior and their application to heath psychology. *Psychology and Health, 13,* 735-740.

Ajzen, I., & Fishbein, M. (1969). The prediction of behavioral intentions in a choice situation. *Journal of Experimental Social Psychology, 5,* 400-416.

Ajzen, I., & Fishbein, M. (1980) *Understanding Attitudes and predicting social behavior,* Englewood Cliffs, NJ: Prentice-Hall.

Armitage, C. J., & Conner, M. (2001). Efficacy of the theory of planned behaviour: A meta-analytic review. *British Journal of Social Psychology, 40,* 471-499.

Austin, J., T., & Vancouver, J. B. (1996). Goal constructs in psychology: Structure, process, and content. *Psychological Review, 120,* 338-375.

Bagozzi, R. P. (1992). The self-regulation of attitudes, intentions and behavior. *Social Psychology Quarterly, 55,* 178-204.

Bagozzi, R. P, & Edwards, E. A. (1998). Goal setting and goal pursuit in the regulation of body weight. *Psychology and Health, 13*, 593-621.

Bandura, A. (1977). Self-efficacy: Towards a unifying theory of behavioral change. *Psychological Review, 84*, 191-215.

Bandura, A. (1997). *Self-efficacy; The exercise of control*, New York: Freeman.

Belloc, N. B., & Breslow, L. (1972). Relationship of physical health status and health practices. *Preventive Medicine, 1*, 409-421.

Carver, C. S., & Scheier, M. F. (1982). Control theory: a useful conceptual framework for personality-social, clinical and health psychology. *Psychological Bulletin, 92*, 111-135.

Carver, C. S., & Scheier, M. F. (1998). *On the self-regulation of behavior*. Cambridge: Cambridge University Press.

Chatzisarantis, N. L. D., Biddle, S. J. H., & Meek, G. A. (1997). A self-determination theory approach to the study of intentions and the intention-behaviour relationship in children's physical activity. *British Journal of Health Psychology, 2*, 343-360.

Conner, M., & Armitage, C. J. (1998). Extending the theory of planned behavior: A review and avenues for further research. *Journal of Applied Social Psychology, 28*, 1429-1464.

Conner, M., Sheeran, P., Norman, P. & Armitage, C. J. (2001). Temporal stability as a moderator of relationships in the theory of planned behaviour. *British Journal of Social Psychology, 39*, 469-493.

Cooke, R. & Sheeran, P. (2001). Predictive validity of properties of attitudes and intentions: A meta-analysis. Joint European Health Psychology Society and BPS Division of Health Psychology Conference. University of St Andrews.

Davidson, A. R., & Morrison, D. M. (1983). Predicting contraceptive behavior from attitudes: A comparison of within- versus between-subjects procedures. *Journal of Personality and Social Psychology, 45*, 997-1009.

Deci, E. L., & Ryan, R. M. (1985). *Intrinsic motivation and self-determination in human behavior*. London: Plenum.

Dijksterhuis, A., & Bargh, J. A. (2001). The preception-behavior expressway: Automatic effects of social perception on social behavior. In M. P. Zanna (Ed.), *Advances in experimental social psychology* (Vol. 33, pp. 1-40). New York: Academic Press.

Dodge, K. A., Asher, S. R., & Pankhurst, J. T. (1989). Social life as a goal-coordination task. In C. Ames & R. Ames (Eds.), *Research on motivation in education: Goals and cognitions* (Vol. 3, pp. 107-135). San Diego, CA: Academic Press.

Eagly, A. H., & Chaiken, S. (1993). *The psychology of attitudes*. San Diego, CA: Harcourt Brace Jovanovich.

Edwards, J. R. (1994). The study of congruence in organizational behavior research: Critique and proposed alternative. *Organizational Behavior and Human Decision Processes, 58*, 51-100.

Fishbein, M. (1980). A theory of reasoned action: Some applications and implications. In H. Howe & M. Page (eds.), *Nebraska symposium on motivation* (Vol. 27, pp. 65-116). Lincoln: University of Nebraska Press.

Fishbein, M. & Ajzen, I. (1975) *Belief, attitude, intention and behavior: An introduction to theory and research*. Reading, MA: Addison-Wesley.

Fishbein, M., Ajzen, I., & Hinkle, (1980). Predictng and understanding women's occupational orientations: Factors underlying choice intentions. In I. Ajzen & M. Fishbein *Understanding attitudes and predicting behavior* (pp 113-129). Englewood-Cliffs, NJ: Prentice-Hall.

Godin, G., & Kok, G. (1996). The theory of planned behavior: A review of its applications to health-related behaviors. *American Journal of Health Promotion, 11*, 97-98.

Gollwitzer, P. M. (1999). Implementation intentions: Strong effects of simple plans. *American Psychologist, 54*, 493-503.

Gollwitzer, P. M., & Moskowitz, G. B. (1996). Goal effects on action and cognition: In E. T. Higgins & A. W. Kruglanski (Eds.), *Social psychology: Handbook of basic principles*. New York: Guilford.

Gollwitzer, P. M., & Schaal, B. (1998). Metacognition in action: The importance of implementation intentions: *Personality and Social Psychology Review, 2*, 124-136.

Griffin, D., Murray, S., & Gonzlez, R. (1999). Difference score correlations in relationship research: A conceptual primer. *Personal Relationships, 6*, 505-518.

Hyland, M. E. (1988). Motivational control theory: an integrative framework. *Journal of Personality and Social Psychology, 55*, 642-651.

Jones, F., Abraham, C., Harris, P., Schulz, J., & Chrispin, C. (2001). From knowledge to action regulation: Modelling the cognitive prerequisites of sunscreen use in Australian and UK samples. *Psychology and Health, 16,* 191-206.

Karoly, P. (1998). Expanding the conceptual range of health self-regulation research: a commentary. *Psychology and Health, 13*, 741-746.

Kuhl, J. (1985). From cognition to behavior: Perspectives for future research on action control. In J. Kuhl & J. Beckman (Eds.), *Action control: From cognition to behavior* (pp. 267-276). New York: Springer-Verlag.

Kuhl, J. (1992). A theory of self regulation: action versus state orientation, self-discrimination and some applications. *Applied Psychology: An International Review, 41*, 97-129.

Locke, E. A., Shaw, K. N., Saari, L. M., Latham, G. P. Goal setting and task performance: 1969-1980. *Psychological Bulletin, 90*, 125-152.

Miller, G., A., Galanter, E., & Pribram, K., H. (1960) *Plans and the structure of behavior*. New York, Holt.

Milne, S. E., Orbell, S., & Sheeran, P. (in press). Combining motivational and volitional interventions to promote exercise participation: Protection motivation theory and implementation intentions. *British Journal of Health Psychology*.

Orbell, S., Hodgkins, S., & Sheeran, P. (1997). Implementation intentions and the theory of planned behavior. *Personality and Social Psychology Bulletin, 23*, 953-962.

Powers, M. T. (1973). *Behavior: The control of perception*. Chicago: Aldine.

Ryan, R. M., & Connell, J. (1989). Perceived locus of causality and internalization: Examining reasons for acting in two domains. *Journal of Personality and Social Psychology, 57*, 749-761.

Ryan, R. M., Sheldon, K. M., Kasser, T., & Deci, E. L. (1996). All goals are not created equal: An organismic perspective on the nature of goals and their regulation. In P. M. Gollwitzer & J. A. Bargh (Eds.), *The psychology of action* (pp. 7-26). London: Guilford.

Sheeran, P. (2001). *Effects of achievement and affiliation primes on intentions to study and socialise* [Unpublished raw data], University of Sheffield, UK.

Sheeran, P. (2002). Intention-behaviour relations: A conceptual and empirical review. *European Review of Social Psychology, 12*, 1-36.

Sheeran, P., & Abraham, C. (2002). Mediator of Moderators: Temporal Stability of Intention and the Intention-Behavior Relation. *Personality and Social Psychology Bulletin*.

Sheeran, P., Norman, P. & Orbell, S. (1999). Evidence that intentions based on attitudes better predict behaviour than intentions based on subjective norms. *European Journal of Social Psychology, 29*, 403-406.

Sheeran, P., & Orbell, S. (1998). Do intentions predict condom use? Meta-analysis and examination of six moderator variables. *British Journal of Social Psychology, 37*, 231-250.

Sheeran, P., Orbell, S., & Trafimow, D. (1999). Does the temporal stability of behavioral intentions moderate intention-behavior and past behavior-future behavior relations? *Personality and Social Psychology Bulletin, 25*, 721-730.

Sheeran, P., & Taylor, S. (1999). Predicting intentions to use condoms: Meta-analysis and comparison of the theories of reasoned action and planned behavior. *Journal of Applied Social Psychology, 29*, 1624-1675.

122   Planned Behavior

Sheeran, P., & Trafimow, D. (2001). Towards an integration of goal theories and attitude-behavior models (manuscript under review).
Sheldon, K. M., & Elliott, A. J. (1998). Not all personal goals are personal: Comparing autonomous and controlled reasons for goals as predictors of effort and attainment. *Personality and Social Psychology Bulletin, 23*, 915-927.
Sheppard, B. H., Hartwick, J., & Warshaw, P. R. (1988). The theory of reasoned action: a meta-analysis of past research with recommendations for modifications and future research. *Journal of Consumer Research, 15*, 325-343.
Sperber, B. M., Fishbein, M., Ajzen, I. (1980). Predictng and understanding women's occupational orientations: Factors underlying choice intentions. In I. Ajzen & M. Fishbein *Understanding attitudes and predicting behavior* (pp 113-129). Englewood-Cliffs, NJ: Prentice-Hall.
Trafimow, D., & Finlay, K. A. (1996). The importance of subjective norms for a minority of people: Between-subjects and within-subjects analyses. *Personality and Social Psychology Bulletin, 22*, 820-828
Tubbs, M. E. (1986). Goal setting: A meta-analytic examination of the empirical data. *Journal of Applied Psychology, 71*, 474-483.
Vallacher, R. R., & Wegner, D. M. (1985). *A theory of action identification.* Hillsdale, NJ: Erlbaum.
Vallacher, R. R., & Wegner, D. M. (1987). What do people think they are doing? Action identification and human behavior. *Psychological Review, 94*, 3-15.
van der Pligt, J., de Vries, N. K., Manstead, A. S. R., & van Harreveld, F. (2000). The importance of being selective: Weighing the role of attribute importance in attitudinal judgment. In M. P. Zanna (Ed.), *Advances in experimental social psychology* (Vol. 32, pp. 135-200). New York: Academic Press.
Verplanken, B., & Aarts, H. (1999). Habit, attitude, and planned behaviour: Is habit an empty construct or an interesting case of automaticity? In W. Stroebe & M. Hewstone (Eds.), *European review of social psychology* (Vol. 10, pp. 101-134). Chicester, UK: Wiley.
Wight, D. (1992). Impediments to safer heterosexual sex: A review of research with young people. *AIDS Care, 4*, 11-21.
Williams, G. C., Grow, V. M., Freedman, Z. R., Ryan, R. M., & Deci, E.L. (1996). Motivational predictors of weight loss and weight loss maintenance. *Journal of Personality and Social Psychology, 70*, 115-126.

Index

Contributors

Charles Abraham, University of Sussex

Dominic Abrams, University of Kent

Christopher J. Armitage, University of Sheffield

Julie Christian, University of Birmingham

Mark Conner, University of Leeds

David P. French, University of Cambridge

Simon Griffin, University of Cambridge

Wendy Hardeman, University of Cambridge

Susie J. Hennings, University of Cambridge

Ann Louise Kimmonth, University of Cambridge

Brian McMillan, University of Leeds

Jo Mitchell, University of Cambridge

Rory C. O'Connor, University of Stirling

Amanda Rivis, University of Sheffield

Paschal Sheeran, University of Sheffield

Neil Smith, University of Leeds

Stephen Sutton, University of Cambridge

Nicholas J. Wareham, University of Cambridge